Book by
Mark Cabaniss

Music & Lyrics by
Lowell Alexander

Arranged by
Chris Miller

STEELE SPRING
STAGE RIGHTS
www.stagerights.com

M000249090

IN
BEDFORD FALLS

STAGING MIRACLE IN BEDFORD FALLS

Although *Miracle in Bedford Falls* has several scenes listed, it can be staged with minimal sets. For example, Potter's office can be suggested with a few chairs and a simple desk. The Granville House can be depicted with a couch and a few chairs and other simple set dressing. Other scenes can use similar simple set pieces to suggest the scene. The (optional) statue of Henry Potter suggested during the song "Swell" can be a cardboard cutout, or actual *papier Mache* likeness.

One staging approach might be to have the Main Street backdrop and other selected trappings of Main Street remain in tact (or at least partially exposed) throughout the musical while various set pieces are placed in the midst of it, reinforcing being in Bedford Falls throughout the musical.

—*The Authors*

RUN TIME

2 Hours

MUSICAL NUMBERS

ACT I

ACT II

ACT I

SCENE 1
MAIN STREET

It is Christmas Eve Day, 1946. It is the beginning of another day in Bedford Falls, New York, but not just any day. The Townspeople are standing, frozen, in various tableaux around the stage. The first citizen comes to life by tapping his foot, (mirrored by the percussionist's beat from the orchestra) which is soon mirrored by others who also come to life with complementary rhythms: BERT the policeman stands directing traffic with his whistle, which is the "traffic of life" in Bedford Falls. Other characters enter from different parts of the house. There is no actual traffic, but rather a stylized, choreographed opening song where other elements on Main Street fall perfectly into synch with each other: people walking, a Salvation Army bell ringer next to a kettle, a street sweeper with a broom, the horn of a Taxi cab and a young boy who crosses the stage on a bicycle with a bell. HENRY POTTER is wheeled by in his wheelchair by one of his goons. He is reading a newspaper, looks up long enough to register disapproval as he is wheeled off. Soon, the plaintive musical beginning develops into an energetic, swinging 1940's celebration of Christmas.

SONG #2: CHRISTMAS IS COMING TO TOWN

ALL:
THERE'S A TAXI CAB
BEEPIN' DOWN THE STREET
AND THE WHOLE BACK SEAT IS FULL OF PACKAGES.
WON'T BE LONG 'TIL SNOW'S FALLIN' DOWN.
CHRISTMAS IS COMING TO TOWN.

THERE'S A TRAFFIC COP
WHISTLE BLOWING STRONG
SORTA LIKE A SONG FOR THE HOLIDAYS
KIND OF MAKES A BEAUTIFUL SOUND
CHRISTMAS IS COMING TO TOWN

ALL (CONT'D):
IT'S A WINTER RHYTHM
PEOPLE GOIN' 'BOUT THE BUSINESS OF LIVIN'
GONNA FIND SOME CHEER
THIS TIME OF YEAR

AT THE FIVE AND DIME
BY THE FROSTED GLASS
LADY RINGS A BRASS SALVATION ARMY BELL
HEY, THE SEASON'S ROLLIN' AROUND

CHRISTMAS IS COMIN' TO TOWN
CHRISTMAS IS COMIN'
CHRISTMAS IS COMIN'
CHRISTMAS IS COMIN' TO TOWN

> *Near the end of the opening song, when the cast is finished singing, the "rhythm of Bedford Falls" continues (whistle, tapping, street sweeping, etc.) and tapers off slowly as the street lights begin to illuminate and night falls on Bedford Falls. The backdrop is a beautiful scenic of Bedford Falls with key local locations depicted: A church, Gower's Drugstore, a few homes (including the Bailey house) and the Bedford Garage. The opening song segues into underscore of the carol "O Come, All Ye Faithful" which is reflective; tender. The cast exits slowly as the focus is shifted to the backdrop. As several voices are heard praying from offstage, their corresponding locations are highlighted on the backdrop (or street set).*

SONG #2A: UNDERSCORE (O COME, ALL YE FAITHFUL)

> *Gower's Drugstore is lit.*

GOWER'S VOICE: I owe everything to George Bailey. Help him, dear Father.

> *A home is lit.*

BERT'S VOICE: He never thinks about himself, God, that's why he's in trouble.

> *Bailey house is lit.*

MARY'S VOICE: I love him, dear Lord. Watch over him tonight.

JANIE'S VOICE: Please, God. Something's the matter with daddy.

ZUZU'S VOICE: Please bring daddy back.

The final location fades on the backdrop and the Music 2a. segues to Music 2b. (harp-like piano sounds). A few prominent stars begin to twinkle in synch to their respective dialog. These stars are "heavenly higher-ups" and are speaking of their concern about one of Bedford Falls' leading citizens, George Bailey.

SONG #2B: CELESTIAL SOUNDS

FRANKLIN'S VOICE: Hello, Joseph. Trouble?

JOSEPH'S VOICE: Looks like we'll have to send someone to Earth. A lot of people are asking for help for a man named George Bailey.

FRANKLIN'S VOICE: George Bailey. Yes, tonight's his crucial night. You're right, we'll have to send someone down immediately. Whose turn is it?

Underscore ends.

JOSEPH'S VOICE: That's why I came to see you, sir. It's that clock-maker's turn again.

FRANKLIN'S VOICE: Oh... Clarence. Hasn't got his wings yet, has he? We've passed him up right along.

JOSEPH'S VOICE: Because, you know, sir, he's got the I.Q. of a rabbit.

FRANKLIN'S VOICE: Yes, but he's got the faith of a child. Joseph, send for Clarence.

A smaller star "flies in" on the backdrop. It twinkles as CLARENCE speaks.

CLARENCE'S VOICE: You sent for me, sir?

FRANKLIN'S VOICE: Yes, Clarence. A man down on earth needs our help.

CLARENCE'S VOICE: Splendid! Is he sick?

FRANKLIN'S VOICE: No, worse. He's discouraged. At exactly ten-forty-five p.m. tonight, Earth time, that man will be thinking seriously of throwing away God's greatest gift.

CLARENCE'S VOICE: Oh, dear, dear! His life! Then I've only an hour to dress. What are they wearing now?

FRANKLIN'S VOICE: You will spend that hour getting acquainted with George Bailey.

CLARENCE'S VOICE: Sir, if I should accomplish this mission, might I perhaps win my wings? I've been waiting for over two hundred years now, sir... and people are beginning to talk.

FRANKLIN'S VOICE: What's that book you've got there?

CLARENCE'S VOICE: "The Adventures of Tom Sawyer."

FRANKLIN'S VOICE: Clarence, you do a good job with George Bailey, and you'll get your wings.

CLARENCE'S VOICE: Oh, thank you, sir. Thank you.

JOSEPH'S VOICE: Pay attention, Clarence, and you'll know everything you need to know about him.

CLARENCE'S VOICE: Yes, sir.

JOSEPH'S VOICE: Now, keep your eyes open. See the town?

CLARENCE'S VOICE: Where? I don't see a thing.

JOSEPH'S VOICE: Oh, I forgot. You haven't got your wings yet. Now look, I'll help you out. Concentrate. Begin to see something?

SONG #2C: *CELESTIAL SOUNDS (REPRISE)*

Harp-like sounds are again heard as the lights fade up on Gower's Drugstore (located center) and JOSEPH and CLARENCE "materialize" on stage and stand stage right of the drugstore unit. A young GEORGE enters the drugstore enthusiastically. He is whistling and removes his coat and hangs it up behind the counter and puts on his apron.

SCENE 2
GOWER'S DRUGSTORE

CLARENCE: Why, yes. This is amazing. Who's that young man?

JOSEPH: That's your problem, George Bailey.

CLARENCE: A boy?

JOSEPH: That's him when he was twelve, back in 1919.

The lights fade on the Drugstore. GEORGE exits.

(Crossing center; Clarence follows)

Now, there are two important events which occurred to George when he was a boy which you need to keep in mind, Clarence.

CLARENCE *(pulling out a small note pad and pencil)*: Yes, sir.

JOSEPH: One was when his young brother, Harry, fell through the ice while they were playing and almost drowned. George jumped in and saved him. And ever since, George has had a bad ear... all that icy water and... well, you understand.

CLARENCE *(writing on the note pad)*: Brother falls through ice... George saves him... bad ear. Got it.

JOSEPH *(crossing to left of the drugstore unit; Clarence follows)*: The other event came a few months later.

The lights fade up on the drugstore. GEORGE enters wearing his apron and baseball cap.

George used to work after school in Mr. Gower's Drugstore. One day, Mr. Gower's only son died of influenza. It was a terrible blow and Mr. Gower tried to lose his grief in whiskey.

Lights fade on JOSEPH and CLARENCE. MR. GOWER enters. He is bleary-eyed, unshaven and chewing an old unlit cigar. His manner is gruff and mean. It is evident he has been drinking.

MR. GOWER *(drunkenly)*: George! George! Where's Mrs. Blaine's box of capsules?

GEORGE: Capsules...

MR. GOWER *(angrily)*: Did you hear what I said?

GEORGE *(frightened)*: Yes, sir, I...

MR. GOWER: Don't you know that boy's been very sick? What kind of tricks are you playing, anyway?

GOWER grabs GEORGE by the shoulders and starts shaking him.

Why didn't you deliver them right away?

GEORGE: You're hurting me, Mr. Gower!

MR. GOWER *(continuing the assault)*: You lazy loafer!

GEORGE *(in tears)*: Mr. Gower, you don't know what you're doing. You put something wrong in those capsules. I know you're unhappy. You got that telegram, and you're upset. You put something bad in those capsules. It wasn't your fault, Mr. Gower...

> *GEORGE pulls the little box out of his pocket. GOWER savagely rips it away from him, breathing heavily, staring at the boy venomously.*

Just look and see what you did. Look at the bottle you took the powder from. It's poison! I tell you it's poison! I know you feel bad...

> *GOWER tears open the package, shakes the powder out of one of the capsules, cautiously tastes it, then abruptly throws the whole mess to the counter and turns to look at GEORGE again. The boy is whimpering, hurt, frightened. Gower steps toward him.*

Don't hurt me again!

> *This time, GOWER sweeps the boy to him in a hug, and sobbing hoarsely crushes the boy in his embrace. GEORGE is crying too.*

MR. GOWER *(sobbing)*: Oh, George, George...

> *The lights fade on the drugstore. MR. GOWER and GEORGE exit. Lights up on JOSEPH and CLARENCE, who cross to center.*

JOSEPH: Well, Clarence, that was George Bailey as a boy. When he grew up he wanted to go to college, but there just wasn't the money. So he worked four years in the Building and Loan Association.

CLARENCE: Building and Loan Association?

JOSEPH: Oh, I forgot to tell you. George's father was in the building and loan business... along with George's Uncle Billy. High ideals and a low bank account. Anyway, George worked for his father and saved enough to send him to the university. That summer, though, he was going to Europe. Got a job on a cattle boat. Going to do a little traveling before college.

> *As JOSEPH and CLARENCE cross to Stage Right of the drugstore unit, lights fade up again on the drugstore. An adult GEORGE BAILEY is examining a piece of luggage. Across the counter stands JOE showing the suitcase.*

JOE: Here's the suitcase for your trip, George.

GEORGE: Nope. Nope. Nope. Now look, Joe. Now look, I... I want a big one.

SONG #3: UNDERSCORE – ANGELS

> Suddenly, in action, as GEORGE stands with his arms outstretched in illustration, he and JOE freeze. As they hold the pose, JOSEPH and CLARENCE continue.

CLARENCE: What did you stop it for?

JOSEPH: I want you to take a good look at that face.

CLARENCE: Who is it?

JOSEPH: George Bailey.

CLARENCE: Oh, you mean the kid that got shook up by the druggist?

JOSEPH: That's the kid.

CLARENCE: It's a good face. I like it. I like George Bailey.

> Underscore ends

GEORGE (springing to life again): Big... see! I don't want one for one night. I want something for a thousand and one nights, with plenty of room for labels from Italy and Baghdad, Samarkand.

JOE: I see, a flying carpet, huh? I don't suppose you'd like this old second-hand job, would you?

> He brings a large suitcase from under the counter.

GEORGE: Now you're talking. Gee whiz, I could use this as a raft in case the boat sank. How much does this cost?

JOE: No charge.

GEORGE: That's my trick ear, Joe. It sounded as if you said no charge.

JOE: That's right. It's a little present from Mr. Gower. He picked it out himself. He wanted to surprise you with this.

GEORGE (admiring the bag): He did? Whatta you know about that... my old boss...

JOE: What boat you sailing on?

GEORGE: I'm working across on a cattle boat.

JOE: A cattle boat?

GEORGE (sarcastically): Okay, I like cows.

> Introduction to Music Song #4 begins.

JOE: Good luck, George. Be sure to remember old Bedford Falls.

GEORGE (shaking Joe's hand): Thanks, Joe. You bet I will. Now, if you'll excuse me, my good man, I've got some dreams I need to attend to.

SCENE 3
MAIN STREET

GEORGE exits onto Main Street where several people, including UNCLE BILLY, VIOLET, ERNIE and BERT are milling about.

BERT: Hey, George! What's with the suitcase?

GEORGE:
  I'M SHAKIN' THE DUST FROM BEDFORD FALLS
  OFF OF MY SHOES, IT'S A BIG WORLD OUT THERE
  IT'S LONDON OR BUST WHERE CASTLE WALLS
  WAIT WITH A REGAL REFINED CHARM AND FLAIR
  GOT MY SUITCASE FILLED WITH EXPECTATIONS
  IT'S LONG OVERDUE
  I'M SHAKIN' THE DUST IT'S LONDON OR BUST
  I'M GIVING THE BRUSH TO THESE SMALL-TOWN BLUES
VIOLET:
  HE'S SHAKIN' THE DUST FROM BEDFORD FALLS
  OFF OF HIS SHOES, HE'S GONNA BREATHE THE AIR.
  IT'S PARIS OR BUST WHERE PARASOLS
  SPIN IN THE SUN WITH CERTAIN SAVOIR FAIRE.
BERT:
  GOT HIS SUITCASE FILLED WITH EXPECTATIONS
  SO WE'LL SAY "ADIEU"
  HE'S SHAKIN' THE DUST IT'S PARIS OR BUST
  HE'S GIVING THE BRUSH TO THESE SMALL-TOWN BLUES

Music vamps under dialog.

UNCLE BILLY: Avast, there, Captain Cook. You got your sea legs yet?

VIOLET: Parlez-vous Francais? Hey, send us some of them picture postcards, will you, Georgie?

GEORGE: Hello, Violet! Hey, you look good. That's some dress you got on there.

VIOLET: Oh, this old thing? Well, I only wear it when I don't care how I look.

UNCLE BILLY: Hey, George, don't take any plugged nickels.

ERNIE: Hey, George, your suitcase is leaking.

GEORGE: Who cares!

GEORGE puts the suitcase down and dances on top of it with other bits of business while the townspeople sing.

> *The entire cast joins around him culminating in a glorious celebration of George's new life.*

ALL:
HE'S SHAKIN' THE DUST FROM BEDFORD FALLS
OFF OF HIS SHOES, HE'S GONNA SEE THE SIGHTS
IT'S VENICE OR BUST WHERE GONDOLAS
FLOAT THROUGH CANALS BENEATH THE CITY LIGHTS

GEORGE:
GOT MY SUITCASE FILLED WITH EXPECTATIONS
IT'S LONG OVERDUE

ALL:
HE'S SHAKIN' THE DUST IT'S VENICE OR BUST
HE'S GIVING THE BRUSH TO THESE SMALL-TOWN BLUES

GEORGE:
I'M SHAKIN' THE DUST
(Speaking)
It's the whole world, or bust!

ALL:
HE'S GIVING THE BRUSH...

GEORGE & ALL:
TO THESE SMALL-TOWN BLUES!

SONG #4A: SHAKIN' THE DUST (PLAYOFF)

JOSEPH and CLARENCE enter stage left.

CLARENCE: So George is getting ready to leave Bedford Falls for his new life.

JOSEPH: That's right, Clarence. But his father asks him to consider staying in Bedford Falls to help with the Building and Loan, but George will have no part of it. Says he's not sure he can handle the business of "nickels and dimes".

CLARENCE: Well, is he on that boat yet to see the world?

JOSEPH: Not before he stops by a school dance with his brother Harry.

CLARENCE: Why do I need to know about the school dance?

JOSEPH: Because it's at this dance that George really takes a shine to Mary Hatch.

CLARENCE: Who's she?

JOSEPH: You'll see. Watch closely now, Clarence.

The lights fade up on the next scene.

SONG #5: UNDERSCORE – THE HIGH SCHOOL GYM

SCENE 4

THE HIGH SCHOOL GYM

JOSEPH and CLARENCE exit as the lights reveal the High School Gymnasium. People are milling about, mingling, laughing and having a good time. GEORGE and HARRY BAILEY enter and SAM WAINWRIGHT comes in behind them to surprise them.

SAM *(wiggling his hands in his ears):* Surprise! Surprise! Hee-haw!

GEORGE swings around, delighted to hear a familiar voice.

GEORGE: Oh, oh. Sam Wainwright! How are you? When did you get here?

SAM: Oh, this afternoon. I thought I'd give the kids a treat.

GEORGE: Old college graduate now, huh?

SAM: Yeah, old Joe College Wainwright, they call me. Well, freshman, looks like you're going to make it after all.

GEORGE: Yep.

SAM sees HARRY and immediately turns his attention to him.

SAM: Harry! You're the guy I want to see. Coach has heard all about you.

HARRY: He has?

SAM: Yeah. He's followed every game and his mouth's watering. He wants me to find out if you're going to come along with us.

HARRY: Well, I gotta make some dough first. I'm going to work at the Building and Loan while big brother here gets an education.

SAM: Well, you better make it fast. We need great ends like you... *(Indicating George)* ...not broken down old guys like this one.

GEORGE and SAM wiggle their fingers in their ears, saluting each other.

GEORGE: Hee-haw!

SAM: Hee-haw!

VIOLET enters and crosses to GEORGE.

VIOLET: Hey, George...

GEORGE: Hello, Violet.

VIOLET: How 'bout a dance?

MARTY HATCH comes over to GEORGE interrupting his conversation with VIOLET.

MARTY: Hey, George!

GEORGE: Hiya, Marty. Well, it's old home week.

MARTY: Do me a favor, will you, George?

GEORGE: What's that?

MARTY: Well, you remember my kid sister, Mary?

GEORGE: Oh, yeah, yeah.

MARTY: Dance with her, will you?

GEORGE: Oh... me? Oh, well, I feel funny enough already, with all these kids.

> VIOLET is becoming annoyed.

MARTY: Aw, come on. Be a sport. Just dance with her one time and you'll give her the thrill of her life.

GEORGE: Well, I don't...

MARTY (calling across stage): Hey, sis.

> MARY, who has been cornered by FREDDIE who has been chatting with her, turns toward MARTY. She is holding a glass of punch. Standing next to Freddie is MICKEY.

GEORGE: Well, excuse me, Violet. Don't be long, Marty. I don't want to be...

> GEORGE suddenly stops mid-sentence as he sees MARY and stares at her. George crosses to MARY. MARTY follows behind. VIOLET exits in a huff.

MARTY: You remember George? This is Mary. Well, I'll be seeing you.

> MARTY joins the crowd.

GEORGE: Well... well... well...

FREDDIE (to Mary): Now, to get back to my story, see...

> MARY, not even looking at FREDDIE hands her punch cup to MICKEY, and she and GEORGE start dancing.

Hey, this is my dance!

GEORGE: Oh, why don't you stop annoying people!

FREDDIE: Well, I'm sorry. Hey!

> FREDDIE turns abruptly and joins the crowd. MICKEY wanders downstage to another part of the gym.

GEORGE: Well, hello.

MARY: Hello. You look at me as if you didn't know me.

GEORGE: Well, I don't.

MARY: You've passed me on the street almost every day.

GEORGE: Me?

MARY: Uh-huh.

GEORGE: That was a little girl named Mary Hatch. That wasn't you.

GEORGE and MARY continue to dance slowly and romantically across the stage. MICKEY is standing downstage and motions for FREDDIE to join him. FREDDIE crosses to him with a "What's up?" look on his face.

MICKEY: So George Bailey stole the one you had your eye on tonight, huh? Do I detect a bit of jealously?

FREDDIE: I'll take care of him somehow.

MICKEY: Well, did you know there's a swimming pool under this floor? (holding up a key) And did you know that I've got the key to the switch that causes this floor to open up? And did you further know that George Bailey is dancing close to the crack which we can open up?

FREDDIE: Yeah, but the floor opens up so slowly, they'll never fall in.

MICKEY: Not if we turn out the lights. I know where that switch is, too!

FREDDIE *(with a vengeance)*: I say we get this party really going.

FREDDIE grabs the key from MICKEY and dashes offstage. MICKEY follows. Meanwhile, GEORGE and MARY continue to dance toward Left Center. A whistle is heard. Music 5 stops. GEORGE and MARY stop dancing. HARRY moves center, whistle in hand.

HARRY: Ladieeeees and gentlemen... oh yez, oh yez... it's time for the big Charleston contest! Those not tapped by the judges will remain on the floor. Let's go!

SONG #6: STEP TO THE MUSIC

GEORGE and MARY shrug as if to say "Why not?" and begin dancing, along with several other couples. A follow spot swirls crazily around the dance floor adding to the excitement of the contest.

ALL:
DANCE...
DANCE...
C'MON, GET OUT, GET UP, GET ON YOUR FEET AND
DANCE...
DANCE... C'MON AND CUT A RUG AND DANCE WITH ME

STEP TO THE MUSIC, KICK UP YOUR HEELS
SWAY AND TWIRL AND SPIN AND WHIRL AND...
SWING TO THE RHYTHM, PUT YOUR FEET IN FLIGHT
STEP TO THE MUSIC, STEP TO THE MUSIC
STEP TO THE MUSIC TONIGHT!

WOMAN: Look! The floor! It's opening up!

MAN *(pointing off left)*: And look at that pool down there!

> *Several of the crowd members hear the exclamations and point off left ad libbing "Watch out!", "There's the pool!", etc. GEORGE and MARY are so busy dancing they don't notice anything.*
>
> *The music crescendos and modulates into a fun, fast Charleston dance number. GEORGE and MARY are eventually the only couple still dancing as the others have been eliminated.*

ALL:
DANCE...
DANCE...
C'MON, GET OUT, GET UP, GET ON YOUR FEET AND
DANCE...
DANCE... C'MON AND CUT A RUG AND DANCE WITH ME
STEP TO THE MUSIC, KICK UP YOUR HEELS
SWAY AND TWIRL AND SPIN AND WHIRL AND...
SWING TO THE RHYTHM, PUT YOUR FEET IN FLIGHT
STEP TO THE MUSIC, STEP TO THE MUSIC
STEP TO THE MUSIC TONIGHT!

> *Suddenly, there's a blackout. Several people scream and laugh. GEORGE and MARY quickly exit Stage Left. The follow spot continues roaming the stage in a random pattern adding to the confusion. Mary suddenly screams offstage and a splashing SFX is heard. The lights come back on full as the chorus sings the final tag:*

C'MON AND CUT A RUG AND DANCE WITH ME!

> *Blackout.*

SONG #6A: STEP TO THE MUSIC (PLAYOFF)

SCENE 5

A STREET IN BEDFORD FALLS

GEORGE and MARY enter Stage Left, in front of the curtain, walking leisurely. They are both wearing oversized robes.

GEORGE & MARY:
"BUFFALO GALS, CAN'T YOU COME OUT TONIGHT.
CAN'T YOU COME OUT TONIGHT.
CAN'T YOU COME OUT TONIGHT.
BUFFALO GALS CAN'T YOU COME OUT TONIGHT
AND DANCE BY THE LIGHT OF THE MOON."

GEORGE: You should have seen the commotion in that locker room after everyone jumped into that pool. I had to knock down three people to get these robes.

MARY: Do I look as funny as you do?

They stop at center.

GEORGE: You... you look wonderful. You know, if it wasn't me talking I'd say you were the prettiest girl in town.

MARY: Well, why don't you say it?

GEORGE: I don't know. Maybe I will say it. *(Changing the subject, looking out over the audience's heads and motioning)* Hey, look where we are.

MARY *(fondly)*: Oh, the old Granville House.

GEORGE: Hey, watch. I gotta throw a rock.

GEORGE pantomimes picking up a rock from the street.

MARY: Oh, no, don't. I love that old house.

GEORGE: Don't you know about deserted houses? You see, you make a wish and then try to break some glass.

MARY: Oh, no, George, don't. It's full of romance, that old place. I'd like to live in it someday.

GEORGE: In there? I wouldn't live in it as a ghost. Now watch... right on the second floor there.

GEORGE pantomimes throwing the rock in his hand over the audience's heads. Glass breaking SFX is heard.

Hey... how 'bout that, huh? Broke a window in one shot!

MARY: What'd you wish, George?

GEORGE: Well, not just one wish. A whole hatful, Mary. I know what I'm going to do tomorrow and the next year and the year after that. I'm shaking the dust of this crummy little town off my feet and I'm going to see the world. Italy, Greece, the Parthenon, the Coliseum. Then I'm coming back here and go to college and see what they know... and then I'm gonna build things.

> *As he talks, MARY has been listening intently. She then stoops down and picks up a rock.*

GEORGE (CONT'D): Are you gonna throw a rock?

> *MARY pantomimes throwing a rock over the audience's heads. Again, the glass breaking SFX is heard.*

Hey, that's pretty good. What'd you wish, Mary?

> *MARY looks at him provocatively, then turns, and shuffles away from him a few steps.*

MARY: Oh, no.

GEORGE: Come on, tell me.

MARY: If I told you, it might not come true.

GEORGE: What is it you want, Mary? What do you want? You want the moon? Just say the word and I'll throw a lasso around it and pull it down.

MARY: I'll take it. Then what?

GEORGE: Well, then you could swallow it and it'd all dissolve, just like an aspirin. And the moonbeams'd shoot out of your fingers and your toes and the ends of your hair.

> *MARY starts to shuffle off farther away from GEORGE.*

Where ya going, Mary?

MARY: Just enjoying the scenery. *(Looking up at the sky)* And sizing up my moon.

> *GEORGE picks up another rock and throws it. No breaking SFX is heard to his dismay. He starts looking around for another rock while MARY begins to sing, lost in her reverie. During "Lucky Star", there's distinctive non-verbal, playful teasing as they pursue each other.*

SONG #7: LUCKY STAR

(Singing)
HEY, IT'S A LOVELY NIGHT
FOR TAKING A LITTLE STROLL OUTSIDE
HEY, THERE'S NO RAIN SO FAR
I MUST HAVE BEEN BORN UNDER A LUCKY STAR

GEORGE:
MY MIND IS REELING,
MY HEART IS FEELING
TOPSY TURVY AND A BIT BIZZARE
I LOST MY BEARINGS

GEORGE (CONT'D):
AND STILL I'M SWEARING
I MUST HAVE BEEN BORN UNDER A LUCKY STAR

MARY (sung simultaneously with George's lyrics below):
HEY, IT'S A STARRY NIGHT.
NOT EVEN A SINGLE CLOUD IN SIGHT.
HEY, THERE'S NO RAIN SO FAR
I MUST HAVE BEEN BORN UNDER A LUCKY STAR.

GEORGE (sung simultaneously with Mary's lyrics above):
MY HEAD IS SPINNIN'
YOU SEE ME GRINNIN'
THINKIN' 'BOUT THE ANGEL THAT YOU ARE
INSIDE I'M DYIN'
THERE'S NO DENYIN'
I MUST HAVE BEEN BORN UNDER A LUCKY STAR
        (Now sings solo)
THE WHOLE TOWN WILL BE WALKING BY

GEORGE & MARY:
SHOCKED BY THE HULLABALOO

GEORGE:
THEY WON'T BELIEVE THEIR EYES WHEN I
LASSO THE MOON FOR YOU

> An offstage man's voice interrupts while the music vamps under the dialog:

MAN (offstage): Hey, sonny! Why don't you kiss her instead of singing her to death?

GEORGE: Want me to kiss her, huh?

MAN: Aw, youth is wasted on the wrong people.

GEORGE: Hey, mister, come back here and I'll show you some kissing that'll put hair back on your head.

> At measure 43, GEORGE takes MARY in his arms and they sing the final duet portion facing the audience. At measure 49, he twirls her out of his arms in a simple dance move while innocently holding onto the sleeve of her robe. As MARY twirls out, her robe slips off and falls to the floor. She is wearing a slip and jumps behind a shrub (or other piece of scenery, center curtain opening or wings).

MARY (sung simultaneously with George's lyrics below):
HEY, IT'S A LOVELY NIGHT
FOR TAKING A LITTLE STROLL OUTSIDE
HEY, THINK I'M IN HIS HEART.
I MUST HAVE BEEN BORN UNDER A LUCKY STAR.

GEORGE *(sung simultaneously with Mary's lyrics above)*:
MY HANDS ARE SHAKIN'
MY HEART IS ACHIN'
I WANNA SHOUT YOUR NAME OUT
NEAR AND FAR.
YOUR EYES ARE GLEAMIN'
COULD I BE DREAMIN'
I MUST HAVE BEEN BORN UNDER A LUCKY STAR

> *GEORGE holds up the robe, smiling devilishly.*

I MUST HAVE BEEN BORN
MARY *(sarcastically popping her head out to sing directly to the audience)*:
HE MUST HAVE BEEN BORN
GEORGE:
I MUST HAVE BEEN BORN
GEORGE & MARY:
UNDER A LUCKY STAR!
MARY: My robe, George. I need my robe.

> *He is about to give her the robe, when a thought strikes him.*

GEORGE: Wait a minute. What am I doing? This is very interesting. A man doesn't get in a situation like this every day.

MARY *(impatiently)*: I'd like to have my robe.

GEORGE: Not in Bedford Falls, anyway. This requires a little thought here.

MARY *(getting mad)*: George Bailey! Give me my robe!

GEORGE: I've heard about things like this, but I've never...

MARY *(desperate)*: I'll call the police.

GEORGE: They're way downtown. They'd be on my side, too.

> *UNCLE BILLY enters excitedly, clearly distressed.*

UNCLE BILLY: George! George! Come home, quick! Something terrible has happened.

GEORGE *(stunned and jolted from his happy mood)*: What? What are you talking about?

UNCLE BILLY *(taking his arm to lead him off)*: Your father's had a stroke. Come on, George, let's hurry.

GEORGE: Mary... Mary, I'm sorry. I've got to go.

> *MARY emerges as GEORGE gives her the robe and she puts it on. UNCLE BILLY and George exit.*

MARY exits. The scene change reveals The Bailey Building and Loan interior. POTTER is seated at the head of the table in a wheelchair. UNCLE BILLY stands at the table with several others who are seated. He is wearing a black armband in mourning.

GEORGE: A factory, huh?

SAM'S VOICE: And here's the point, George. I may have a job for you, unless you're still married to that broken down Building and Loan. Oh, Mary?

MARY *(nervously)*: I'm here.

> *As MARY listens, she turns to look at GEORGE, her lips almost on his lips. Their closeness only continues to intensify their feelings for one another, and they are both feeling it strongly.*

SAM'S VOICE: You tell that guy I'm giving him the chance of a lifetime, you hear? The chance of a lifetime.

MARY *(almost whispering, to George)*: He says it's the chance of a lifetime.

> *GEORGE can stand it no longer. He drops the phone with a crash, grabs MARY by the shoulders and shakes her. Mary begins to cry.*

GEORGE *(fiercely)*: Now you listen to me! I don't want any plastics! I don't want any job and I don't want to get married— ever— to anyone! You understand that? I want to do what I want to do. And you're... you're...

> *He pulls her to him in a fierce embrace. Two meant for each other find themselves in tearful ecstasy.*

Oh, Mary... Mary...

> *They kiss.*

MARY: George... George...

GEORGE: Mary...

> *The lights fade on GEORGE and MARY as they continue their passionate embrace. They exit.*

SONG #8A: CHANGE OF SCENE (WEDDING MARCH)

> *CLARENCE and JOSEPH enter and cross to Downstage Center as the scene changes.*

CLARENCE: So George Bailey and Mary Hatch were...

JOSEPH: Yes. George and Mary were married. And just as they were headed for their honeymoon, they ran smack into the financial panic of 1932.

CLARENCE: Financial panic? What financial panic?

JOSEPH: The Great Depression, Clarence. And at the Bailey Building and Loan, like a lot of other banks, there were a lot of frantic people clamoring for their savings.

CLARENCE: Oh, no. What happened to the Building and Loan? Did they make it?

SCENE 8

THE BUILDING AND LOAN

The lights fade up partially on the Building and Loan.
GEORGE is at the front facing a nervous crowd. UNCLE BILLY,
COUSIN TILLY and COUSIN EUSTACE are standing behind
him.

JOSEPH: Well, there was a crowd gathered in the lobby wanting their money back. And the charter of the Building and Loan said that if they weren't able to stay open until six p.m., the state could close them down.

CLARENCE and JOSEPH exit as the lights fade up full on the
Building and Loan. The crowd noise swells to a dull roar
asking "Where's My Money?" "I want my money!" etc.
GEORGE raises his voice to bring them to order.

GEORGE: Now just a minute! Now please, calm down and listen to me, please.

The crowd quiets.

MAN: How about our money, George? Where's our money?

GEORGE: Now c'mon, wait a minute. Listen to me. Now, you're thinking about this place all wrong. Your money's not here.

The crowd roars again.

(Calming them again)

Now wait a minute! Let me tell you, let me tell you.

The crowd quietens again.

Your money's in people's houses. In Joe's house... *(Motioning to one of the men)* ...right next to yours *(Motioning to another)* And in the Kennedy house and Mrs. Macklin's house, and a hundred others. Now, what are you going to do? Foreclose on them?

TOM: I got two hundred and forty-two dollars in here, and two hundred and forty two dollars isn't going to break anybody.

RANDALL rushes in and makes his way up to TOM.

RANDALL: I got my money! Old man Potter's taking over the bank. He'll pay you fifty cents on every dollar!

MARY enters.

CROWD *(ad lib)*: Fifty cents on the dollar! That sounds great! Let's go!

TOM: Let's take our shares to Potter! Half is better than nothing!

TOM, RANDALL and the others start to exit. GEORGE runs in
front of them to block their exit.

GEORGE: Now wait a minute! Please, folks! I beg of you not to do this thing. If Potter ever gets hold of this Building and Loan there'll never be another decent house built in this town. He's already got charge of the bank.

GEORGE (CONT'D): He's got the bus line. He's got the department stores. And now he's after us. Why? Because we're cutting in on his business and he wants to keep you living in his slums and paying the kind of rent he decides. Now, we can get through this thing all right. But we've got to stick together.

MAN: I've got doctor bills to pay.

WOMAN: I can't feed my kids on faith!

MARY rushes in, holding up a roll of bills and calls out.

MARY: How much do you need? *(To George as she gives him the money)* Here, George. You told me to hang on to it. It would have made a nice honeymoon and furniture, too.

GEORGE *(to the crowd)*: Hey! I got two thousand dollars! This'll tide us over until the bank reopens. All right, Tom, how much do you need?

TOM *(doggedly)*: Two hundred and forty dollars!

GEORGE: Aw, Tom, just enough to tide you over.

TOM: I'll take two hundred and forty dollars.

GEORGE starts to rapidly count out the money.

GEORGE: There you are. Okay, now, Ed... what'll it take till the bank reopens? What do you need?

ED: Well, I suppose twenty dollars.

GEORGE: Now we're talking! Thanks, Ed. All right, now, Mrs. Davis, how much do you want?

MRS. DAVIS: Could I have seventeen-fifty?

GEORGE: Seventeen...

He kisses her on her forehead and then starts counting out her cash. The lights fade to half as CLARENCE and JOSEPH are heard voiceover. The crowd and MARY exit as CLARENCE and JOSEPH speak.

CLARENCE'S VOICE: Well, did he make it?

JOSEPH'S VOICE: He surely did. Didn't make anyone sign anything. He told them he knew they would all pay it back when they could.

Lights fade up. GEORGE, UNCLE BILLY, COUSIN TILLY and COUSIN EUSTACE are nervously watching the wall clock.

SONG #8B: CLOCK UNDERSCORE

UNCLE BILLY *(excitedly)*: We're going to make it, George. They'll never close us up today!

GEORGE *(counting the clock down)*: Five... four... three... two... one... Bingo! We made it!

Everyone cheers. UNCLE BILLY takes a whiskey bottle and four glasses from a desk drawer and pours drinks for everyone.

GEORGE (CONT'D): Look... *(He holds up two one dollar bills)* We're still in business! We've still got two bucks left! Let's have some of that, Uncle Billy. We're a couple of financial wizards.

They all pick up their glasses for a toast.

UNCLE BILLY: A toast!

They all raise their glasses.

GEORGE: Yes... a toast to Papa Dollar and Mama Dollar, and if you want the old Building and Loan to stay in business, you better have a family real quick. So get busy!

GEORGE puts the dollar bills in his pocket. UNCLE BILLY, COUSIN EUSTACE and COUSIN TILLY ad lib hearty agreement as they sip their drinks.

COUSIN TILLY: And here's to what turned out to be a wonderful day!

COUSIN EUSTACE *(quickly adding her toast)*: And to a wonderful new life for the newlyweds!

ALL: Here here! I'll certainly drink to that!

GEORGE sings as he pours whiskey into UNCLE BILLY's glass, and then his own, after he drinks his glass he picks up the bottle and carries it with him throughout the song.

SONG #9: IT'S A WONDERFUL LIFE

GEORGE:
NO MORE PLANS FOR TODAY ON THE DOCKET.
GOT TWO ONE DOLLAR BILLS IN MY POCKET.

UNCLE BILLY:
THINGS ARE AS THEY SHOULD BE
TODAY LIFE HAS BEEN GOOD TO ME.
IT'S A WONDERFUL LIFE!
IT'S REMARKABLY ASTOUNDING EVERY MINUTE.
IT'S A WONDERFUL LIFE.
IT'S A TREASURE AND A PLEASURE TO BE IN IT.

GEORGE:
IT'S PECULIAR AND QUITE CRAZY, UNPREDICTABLY AMAZING.
IT'S A WILD AND RAGING RIDE, A 'ROUND THE CLOCK SURPRISE

GEORGE has the bottle in hand and drinks as the others sing the last line.

BILLY, EUSTICE & TILLY:
IT'S A WONDERFUL, WONDERFUL LIFE!
UNCLE BILLY:
OUR LIMIT IS THE SKY.
(Speaking)
And here's a toast to you, sir!
GEORGE:
THE WAY I SEE THINGS NOW...
ALL:
WE'VE GOT A BRAND NEW FUTURE!

> *UNCLE BILLY sings as GEORGE takes another swig. The phone rings and COUSIN TILLY answers.*

COUSIN TILLY: George, there's a call for you. It's Mrs. Bailey.

GEORGE: Mrs. Bailey... why's Mom calling me?

COUSIN TILLY *(emphatically)*: No... the new Mrs. Bailey!

GEORGE: Oh, that's my wife! *(Taking the phone)* Mary? Hello. Listen, dear, I'm sorry about our honeymoon but... what? Come home? A honeymoon at home? What home? Three-twenty Sycamore? Whose home is that? The Waldorf Astoria Hotel, huh? Okay, I'll be right over.

> *He hangs up and leads the group out of the office into the street for a spectacular finish with the entire cast.*

ALL:
IT'S A WONDERFUL LIFE!
IT'S REMARKABLY ASTOUNDING EVERY MINUTE.
IT'S A WONDERFUL LIFE!
IT'S A TREASURE AND A PLEASURE TO BE IN IT.
IT'S DECISIVELY ERRATIC, SO DEPENDABLY DRAMATIC!
IT'S BEGUILING EV'RY DAY, ENLIGHTENING EV'RY NIGHT

> *GEORGE and UNCLE BILLY are arm in arm; George with bottle in hand.*

IT'S A WONDERFUL, WONDERFUL LIFE!
IT'S A WONDERFUL, WONDERFUL LIFE!

> *BLACKOUT.*

SONG #9A: WONDERFUL LIFE (PLAYOFF)

SCENE 9

THE GRANVILLE HOUSE

The scene change reveals the interior of the Old Granville House. The furniture is covered in drop cloths. The house is clearly in need of repair. Rain/thunder SFX is heard. A collection of packing boxes are heaped together in the shape of a small table and covered partially with a checkered table cloth. It is set for two. A champagne bottle and two glasses sit on the "table". Music Song #9a segues into Music Song #10. As the lights come up, MARY is seen straightening things out a bit, getting it just right for GEORGE's arrival later. She sings as she walks quietly around the room.

SONG #10: I AM HOME

MARY:
IN THIS OLD HOUSE
THE ROOF MAY LEAK
THE STAIRS MAY RATTLE
THE FLOORS MAY CREAK
THESE RUN DOWN ROOMS
ARE PLAIN AND BARE
BUT LONG AS MY MAN'S THERE
I AM HOME

HE IS THE SHELTER
THAT COVERS ME
HE IS THE WINDOW THAT OPENS
TO THE WORLD I SEE
AND WHEN I WALK THROUGH HIS HEART'S DOOR
FROM THE RAFTERS TO THE FLOOR
I AM ONLY HIS, WHEREVER HE IS
I AM HOME

A SIMPLE HOUSE
NO FLASH OR STYLE
DON'T NEED A PALACE
TO MAKE ME SMILE
FOR NEXT TO HIM
IT'S ALL SO CLEAR
THAT LONG AS MY MAN'S HERE
I AM HOME

MARY (CONT'D):
> HE IS THE SHELTER
> THAT COVERS ME
> HE IS THE WINDOW THAT OPENS
> TO THE WORLD I SEE
> AND WHEN I WALK THROUGH HIS HEART'S DOOR
> FROM THE RAFTERS TO THE FLOOR
> I AM ONLY HIS, WHEREVER HE IS
> I AM HOME
>
> AND WHEN I WALK THROUGH HIS HEART'S DOOR
> FROM THE RAFTERS TO THE FLOOR
> I AM ONLY HIS, WHEREVER MY MAN IS
> I AM HOME

> *At the end of the vocal, the music continues to play softly as GEORGE enters.*

(Speaking)

Welcome home, Mr. Bailey.

GEORGE *(overcome)*: Well, I'll be... Mary, Mary, where did you...

> *They rush into each other's arms and hold each other in ecstasy.*

Oh, Mary...

MARY: Remember the night we broke the windows in this old house? This is what I wished for.

GEORGE: Darling, you're wonderful.

> *They embrace. Underscore stops. Lights come up on Stage Right to reveal CLARENCE and JOSEPH as the lights fade on GEORGE and MARY. The scene quietly changes during the ensuing dialog.*

CLARENCE: Are you sure we should be here, Joseph? I don't want to intrude.

JOSEPH: Oh, don't be silly, Clarence. They can't see us. But George will see you soon enough.

CLARENCE: So did they move into that old house?

JOSEPH: Oh, yes. It's where they spent their honeymoon on that night and then started housekeeping. And in the years to come, George built BaileyPark... a nice little neighborhood of affordable homes for folks in Bedford Falls.

CLARENCE: Looks like George was busy.

JOSEPH: Yes he was. About two years after George and Mary were married, Old Man Potter asked George to stop over at his office one afternoon.

> *Lights fade on CLARENCE and JOSEPH and they exit.*

SCENE 10

POTTER'S OFFICE

GEORGE is standing across from MR. POTTER at his desk.
Next to POTTER stands his GOON, ready to obey Potter's
every command.

POTTER: Sit down, George, sit down.

GEORGE reluctantly sits.

GEORGE *(nervously)*: Well, I... I suppose I'll find out sooner or later, but just what exactly did you want to see me about?

POTTER *(pleasantly and smoothly)*: George, I'm an old man, and most people hate me. But I don't like them either, so that makes it all even. You know just as well as I do that I run practically everything in this town but the Bailey Building and Loan. You know, also, that for a number of years I've been trying to get control of it... or kill it. But you've been stopping me. In fact, you have beaten me, George, and as anyone in this county can tell you, that takes some doing. Well, I've stated my side very frankly. Now, let's look at your side. Young man, married, making say... forty a week.

GEORGE *(indignantly)*: Forty-five!

POTTER: Forty-five. Forty-five. Out of which, after supporting your mother, and paying your bills, you're able to keep, say ten, if you skimp. A child or two comes along, and you won't even be able to save ten. Now, if you were some ordinary yokel, I'd say you were doing fine. But, George Bailey is not a common yokel. He's an intelligent, ambitious young man... who hates his job... who hates the Building and Loan, almost as much as I do. He's been dying to shake the dust of this town off his feet since he was born but he's trapped. Trapped into frittering his life away playing nursemaid to a lot of garlic-eaters. Do I paint a correct picture, or do I exaggerate?

GEORGE *(mystified)*: What's your point, Mr. Potter?

POTTER: My point is, I want to hire you.

GEORGE *(dumbfounded)*: Hire me?

POTTER: I want you to manage my affairs, run my properties. George, I'll start you out at twenty thousand dollars a year.

GEORGE *(flabbergasted)*: Twenty thousand dollars a year? You're not talking to somebody else around here are you? You know, this is me, you remember me? George Bailey.

POTTER: Oh, yes, George Bailey. Whose ship has just come in... providing he has brains enough to climb aboard.

GEORGE: Well, what about the Building and Loan?

POTTER: Oh, confound it man, are you afraid of success? I'm offering you a three-year contract at twenty thousand dollars a year, starting today. Is it a deal or isn't it?

GEORGE: Well, Mr. Potter... I... I... I know I ought to jump at the chance, but I... I wonder if it would be possible for you to give me twenty-four hours to think it over?

POTTER: Sure, sure. You go on home and talk about it to your wife. In the meantime, I'll draw up the papers.

GEORGE: All right, sir.

POTTER *(offers hand)*: Okay, George?

GEORGE *(taking his hand)*: Okay, Mr. Potter.

> *As they shake hands, GEORGE feels a physical revulsion. POTTER's hand feels like a cold mackerel to him. In that moment of physical contact he knows he could never be associated with this man. George drops his hand with a shudder. He peers intently into Potter's face.*

> *(Vehemently)*

No... no... no... now, wait a minute, here! I don't have to talk to anybody! I know right now, and the answer is no! NO! Doggone it! *(Getting madder all the time)* You sit around here and you spin your little webs and you think the whole world revolves around you and your money. Well, it doesn't, Mr. Potter! In the whole vast configuration of things, I'd say you were nothing but a scurvy little spider...

> *He looks at the GOON, impassive as ever beside POTTER's wheelchair.*

> *(To the Goon)*

And that goes for you, too!

> *Introduction to Music Song #11 begins. GEORGE storms out of the office to Downstage Center as the lights fade on POTTER and his GOON.*

SCENE 11

A STREET IN BEDFORD FALLS

GEORGE *(angry and confused):* What good is it all? What good is it? I was going to shake the dust of this one-horse town off my feet...

SONG #11: ON MY SHOULDERS

(Singing)
THERE'S AN ANGEL WITH A HALO
AND A DEVIL WITH A PIRATE'S GRIN
ON MY SHOULDERS.
AND WHEREVER I AM THEY GO
PLAYING TUG OF WAR BACK AND FORTH AGAIN
ON MY SHOULDERS.
WHAT I WOULDN'T GIVE FOR MY MIND TO BE CLEAR
WITHOUT ANOTHER DAY OF THEM WHISPERING IN MY EARS.

ON MY SHOULDERS THERE ARE CHOICES
AND I DON'T KNOW IF I'M THAT STRONG.
ON MY SHOULDERS THERE ARE VOICES
AND THEY'RE BABBLING ON AND ON ABOUT RIGHT AND WRONG.
LIFE IS TANGLED AT EACH LEVEL
GOT AND ANGEL AND A DEVIL.
AND THE WEIGHT OF THE WORLD
ON MY SHOULDERS.

THERE ARE PEOPLE HERE WHO LOVE ME
BUT I DON'T WANT THEIR HOPES AND DREAMS
ON MY SHOULDERS.
THERE ARE NEIGHBORS HERE WHO TRUST ME
BUT I CAN'T RECALL WHO ASKED THEM ALL TO LEAN
ON MY SHOULDERS.

EVERYTHING I WANT IS RIGHT IN FRONT OF ME
BUT EVERYTHING I AM STILL WON'T LET ME BE.

ON MY SHOULDERS THERE ARE CHOICES
AND I DON'T KNOW IF I'M THAT STRONG.
ON MY SHOULDERS THERE ARE VOICES
AND THEY'RE BABBLING ON AND ON ABOUT RIGHT AND WRONG.
LIFE IS TANGLED AT EACH LEVEL

GEORGE (CONT'D):
GOT AND ANGEL AND A DEVIL.
AND THE WEIGHT OF THE WORLD
ON MY SHOULDERS.

> *A spot comes up on POTTER who sits in his wheelchair*
> *behind GEORGE and beckons to him as he sings:*

POTTER:
I'LL GIVE YOU MONEY, YOU WILL HAVE POWER
YOU'LL FINALLY HAVE SOMETHING TO SHOW
FOR ALL THE HOURS

GEORGE *(simultaneously)*:
(IT'S ALL ON MY SHOULDERS—)

POTTER:
THAT YOU SPENT ON THIS BROKEN DOWN BUILDING AND LOAN
TO PUT THE RIFF RAFF IN THEIR TINY LITTLE HOMES.

> *(Speaking)*

George, come on and take it!

GEORGE: Never!

POTTER:
IT'S HERE BEFORE YOU

> **GEORGE:** *(IT'S ALL ON MY SHOULDERS—)*

POTTER:
YOU CAN SEE THE WORLD
AND THE WORLD WILL NOT IGNORE YOU
EVERY DREAM YOU EVER DREAMED IS IN MY HANDS.

GEORGE: No... I... I... I've got to get out of here!

> *(Singing)*

ON MY SHOULDERS THERE ARE CHOICES
AND I DON'T KNOW IF I'M THAT STRONG.
ON MY SHOULDERS THERE ARE VOICES
AND THEY'RE BABBLING ON AND ON ABOUT RIGHT AND WRONG.
FOR ALL THE MONEY THAT YOU'VE SHOWN ME
I'D DIE A THOUSAND DEATHS BEFORE I LET YOU OWN ME.

POTTER: Ahhh... go back to your riff-raff George Bailey ..you're weak and you're insignificant. You're a loser and you'll always be a loser!

> *Spotlight on POTTER fades. GEORGE crosses to center to*
> *finish the song boldly.*

GEORGE:
IN EVERY WAY EVERY DAY SEEMS UPSIDE DOWN
AS MY MIND AND MY HEART GO ROUND AND ROUND.

GEORGE (CONT'D):
I DON'T KNOW IF I'M STRONG ENOUGH
TO CARRY THIS TOWN ON MY SHOULDERS!

> *At the end of the song, GEORGE collapses on a nearby park bench. MARY enters and rushes to him.*

MARY: George, George! What's the matter? Did you see Mr. Potter?

GEORGE: Yes, yes... I saw him.

MARY: What did he want?

GEORGE *(sluggishly)*: Oh, nothing. I don't know, I... He just talked... talked. Nothing really.

MARY *(putting her arm around him)*: Is everything alright?

GEORGE: Mary, why in the world did you ever a marry a guy like me?

MARY: To keep from being an old maid.

GEORGE: I was going to see the world. I was going to build things. I was going to give you the moon. You could have married Sam Wainwright or anybody else in town.

MARY: I didn't want to marry anybody else in town. I want my baby to look like you.

GEORGE: You didn't even have a honeymoon. I promised you... *(Does a double-take)* ... your what?

MARY: My baby.

GEORGE *(incredulously)*: You mean... Mary, you mean you're on the nest?

MARY: "George Bailey lassoes stork."

GEORGE: Lassoes the stork! You mean you... what is it, a boy or a girl?

> *MARY nods her head happily. They embrace as lights fade on them and they exit as lights come up on CLARENCE and JOSEPH who enter Stage Right.*

SONG #11A: CHANGE OF SCENE (ROCKABYE)

JOSEPH: Well, Mary had her baby, a boy.

CLARENCE: You don't say!

JOSEPH: Then she had another one— a girl.

CLARENCE: Well, what do ya know.

JOSEPH: Day after day she worked away remaking the old Granville house into a home. Night after night George came back late from the office. Potter was bearing down hard. Then came the war. Mary had another baby by then, but still found time to run the USO. Uncle Billy sold war bonds and George's brother, Harry, became a real hero. Shot down 15 planes.

CLARENCE: But George... what about George?

JOSEPH: George was Four-F on account of his bad ear. George fought the battle of Bedford Falls. He was an air-raid warden. On V-E Day he wept and prayed. On V-J Day he wept and prayed again.

CLARENCE: We're getting pretty close to today, aren't we, sir?

JOSEPH: Yes, Clarence. You now know almost everything you need to know about George Bailey. Except what happened that finds him down there at this moment, wanting to die.

CLARENCE *(eagerly)*: Well sir, well?

JOSEPH: Today's the day before Christmas, uh, Earth time. George is pretty excited because they've just received good news about Harry.

SCENE 12
THE BAILEY BUILDING AND LOAN

JOSEPH motions to the Building and Loan set as lights come up revealing it. CLARENCE and Joseph exit. COUSIN TILLY and COUSIN EUSTACE are there, along with MR. CARTER, the Bank Examiner as GEORGE comes bounding in. He is wearing his overcoat and hat and has a newspaper under his arm.

GEORGE: Hey, Tilly! Eustace! Hey look at this newspaper! *(Reading from the paper)* "Commander Harry Bailey decorated by the President." That's my kid brother. The Congressional Medal of Honor!

COUSIN EUSTACE: Gosh, George, gosh!

GEORGE: What do you think about that? 15 enemy planes, and the last one he got was just about to dive into a transport loaded with soldiers. You know what that means? He saved lives... hundreds of lives! Gee whiz... where's Uncle Billy?

COUSIN TILLY: Gone to the bank, George. He's depositing that eight thousand dollars.

GEORGE: Good... good.

GEORGE sees CARTER sitting nearby.

(Sotto voce, to Tilly)

Who's that?

COUSIN TILLY *(sotto voce)*: It's that man again, Mr. Carter, the bank examiner. He wants the accounts payable.

GEORGE: Oh, uh oh... yeah, *(Raising his voice again, crossing to Mr. Carter as he takes off his coat and hat)* Well, good afternoon, Mr. Carter *(Shaking his hand)* Tilly, get the books for Mr. Carter, will ya? *(Showing Mr. Carter the newspaper)* You know, that's my brother's picture there. He shot down 15 enemy planes.

COUSIN TILLY and COUSIN EUSTACE busy themselves as UNCLE BILLY enters frantically. He is disheveled, wearing his overcoat and has an extremely worried look on his face as he makes a beeline to GEORGE.

Uncle... *(He notices his worried look)* What's going on? *(To Mr. Carter)* Uh, will you excuse us for a moment, Mr. Carter?

MR. CARTER nods approval. GEORGE and UNCLE BILLY cross to a "private" part of the room. COUSIN EUSTACE and COUSIN TILLY approach Mr. Carter to chat with him while George speaks with Uncle Billy.

GEORGE: That's the bank examiner over there and he wants the accounts payable.

GEORGE *stops short, suddenly aware of the tragic old eyes looking up at him.*

GEORGE (CONT'D): What's the matter with you?

UNCLE BILLY: George, I don't know what happened to the money.

GEORGE: What do you mean you don't know what happened to the money? You mean today's deposit?

UNCLE BILLY *(sitting)*: I went to Potter's Bank to make the deposit just like I always do. I reached for the envelope in my coat and it wasn't there. I searched every pocket I have and it wasn't there...

GEORGE *(in disbelief)*: Wasn't there? *(Becoming alarmed)* Wasn't there? How can you lose eight thousand dollars Uncle Billy?

UNCLE BILLY *(desperately)*: I don't know, George. I don't know.

GEORGE *(raising his voice)*: Did you put the envelope in your pocket? Did you retrace your steps?

UNCLE BILLY *(confused)*: Yeah... maybe... maybe...

BILLY sits.

GEORGE *(shouts)*: Maybe— maybe! I don't want any maybe. Uncle Billy, we've got to find that money!

UNCLE BILLY *(piteously)*: I'm no good to you, George. I...

GEORGE: Listen to me. Do you have any secret hiding place here in the office? Someplace you could have put it? Someplace to hide the money?

UNCLE BILLY *(exhausted)*: I've looked everywhere. I went over my whole house.

UNCLE BILLY starts sobbing. GEORGE grabs him by the lapels and pulls him up out of his chair.

GEORGE *(harshly)*: Listen to me! Listen to me! Think! Think!

UNCLE BILLY *(sobbing)*: I can't think anymore, George. I can't think anymore. It hurts...

GEORGE's eyes and manner are almost maniacal.

GEORGE *(furiously)*: Where's that money, you stupid, silly old fool? Where's the money? Do you realize what this means? It means bankruptcy and scandal, and prison! That's what it means! One of us is going to jail! Well, it's not going to be me!

SONG #12: CHANGE OF SCENE

GEORGE releases UNCLE BILLY, turns and storms out. The lights fade as Uncle Billy collapses into his chair. All exit. CLARENCE enters and hears JOSEPH's voice.

CLARENCE: Oh, dear Joseph. What happened? What happened to the money?

JOSEPH'S VOICE: A terrible thing, Clarence, terrible. Uncle Billy gave Old Man Potter a newspaper with the good news about Harry Bailey. Uncle Billy had forgotten that he'd put the eight thousand dollars in an envelope folded up in that newspaper. And Potter wasn't about to tell Uncle Billy about the money.

CLARENCE: Where did George go when he left the bank?

JOSEPH: He ran all the way home in the snow to find his whole family involved in Christmas Eve activities.

CLARENCE exits.

SCENE 13

THE GRANVILLE HOUSE

MARY stands next to the Christmas tree decorating it, along with PETE. TOMMY sits on the floor playing with a toy nearby, while JANIE is seated at the piano playing "Hark! The Herald Angels Sing." GEORGE enters.

MARY: Hello, darling.

CHILDREN *(ad lib)*: Hello daddy, hi daddy.

GEORGE sneezes violently.

MARY & CHILDREN: Bless you!

PETE: Mommy says we can stay up till midnight and sing Christmas carols.

TOMMY: Can you sing, Daddy?

MARY *(to George)*: Better hurry and shave. The families will be here soon.

GEORGE: Families! I don't want the families over here!

MARY leads him downstage away from the children.

(Sharply)

Must she keep playing the piano?

MARY: She has to practice for the party tonight. What is it, dear? Another hectic day?

GEORGE *(sarcastically)*: Yeah, another red-letter day for the Baileys.

PETE *(crossing to George)*: Daddy, the Browns next door have a new car. You should see it.

GEORGE *(snapping at him)*: Well, what's the matter with our car? Isn't it good enough for you?

JANIE stops her piano playing momentarily.

PETE: Yes, daddy.

MARY: Run upstairs, Pete. See if Zuzu's alright.

PETE: Okay, Mom.

PETE exits.

GEORGE: Zuzu? What's the matter with Zuzu?

MARY: Oh, she caught a little cold coming home from school. She didn't button up her coat. The doctor says it's nothing serious.

GEORGE: The doctor? Was the doctor here?

MARY: Yes, I called him right away. She's running a teensie temperature. She'll be alright.

GEORGE: It's this drafty old house. I don't know why we don't all have pneumonia. Why did we have to live here in the first place and have all these kids?

MARY *(worried)*: George, what's wrong?

PETE enters with ZUZU, who is wearing

PETE: Daddy, Zuzu won't go to sleep.

GEORGE and MARY cross to ZUZU.

MARY: Zuzu! What are you doing out of bed?

ZUZU: Daddy, will you fix my flower? It's broken.

GEORGE: All right, all right. Give daddy the flower. I'll paste it back together.

ZUZU hands him the loose petals and the flower. He turns his back to Zuzu to tinker with the flower, sticks the loose petals in his pocket in clear view of the audience, then kneels to Zuzu.

There it is, good as new.

MARY: Okay, honey, back to bed now.

MARY kisses ZUZU and sends her off to bed as GEORGE crosses to sit in his chair. JANIE resumes playing the piano. The phone rings.

JANIE & PETE: Telephone.

MARY: I'll get it.

MARY crosses to answer the phone.

Hello. Yes, this is Mrs. Bailey. Oh, thank you, Mrs. Welch. I'm sure she'll be alright. The doctor says she ought to be out of bed in time to have her Christmas dinner.

GEORGE: Is that Zuzu's teacher?

MARY *(hand over mouthpiece)*: Yes.

GEORGE *(crossing to Mary)*: Let me speak to her.

He snatches the phone from MARY.

Hello, Mrs. Welch? This is George Bailey. I'm Zuzu's father. Say, what kind of teacher are you anyway? What do you mean sending her home like that, half naked? Do you realize she'll probably end up with pneumonia on account of you?

MARY *(shocked, taking the phone from him)*: George! Hello, Mrs. Welch. I want to apologize... hello... hello? *(To George)* She's hung up.

GEORGE: I'll hang her up!

GEORGE crosses to sit in his chair and the phone rings again. MARY starts to answer but GEORGE turns immediately and walks to the phone.

(To Mary)

GEORGE (CONT'D): Wait a minute. *(On phone)* Hello? Who is this? Oh, Mr. Welch. Okay, that's fine Mr. Welch. Give me a chance to tell you what I really think about your wife. *(Slight pause)* Oh, you will, huh? Okay, Mr. Welch, any time you think you're man enough... hello? Oh...

> *GEORGE angrily hangs up the receiver and sits in his chair, sharply picking up a newspaper, which he starts to read behind.*

MARY *(confused and worried)*: George...

GEORGE *(shouting, lowering the newspaper)*: Janie, haven't you learned that silly tune yet? You've played it over and over again. Now stop it! *(Getting even louder, standing and throwing the newspaper down)* I said stop it!

> *JANIE immediately stops playing the piano. The room has become ominously quiet, with MARY and the children staring at GEORGE as if he is some unknown wild animal.*

(Breathless)

I'm sorry, Mary. Janie, I'm sorry. I didn't mean... you go on and practice. Pete, I owe you an apology too for snapping at you. I'm sorry. Janie, go on. I told you to practice. *(Shouting again)* Now, go on, play!

> *JANIE starts to cry.*

MARY *(in an outburst)*: George, why must you torture the children? Why don't you...

GEORGE: Mary...

> *GEORGE looks around desperately, then quickly exits.*

SONG #13: UNDERSCORE/I AM HOME (REPRISE)

PETE: Is daddy in trouble?

MARY: Yes, Pete.

JANIE: Shall I pray for him?

MARY: Yes, Janie, pray very hard.

TOMMY: Me, too?

MARY: You too, Tommy. Now hurry children, run to your bedrooms to say your prayers for daddy.

> *The children exit. MARY slowly crosses downstage. She sings haltingly, choking back tears:*

(Singing)
WHERE IS THE SHELTER
THAT COVERS ME?

MARY (CONT'D):
WHERE IS THE WINDOW THAT OPENS
TO THE WORLD I SEE?

The music continues. MARY crosses to the phone, picks up the receiver and speaks. As she speaks, she carries the phone with her and crosses to Downstage Center.

Bedford two-four-seven, please. *(Slight pause)* Hello, Uncle Billy?

MARY begins sobbing and collapses in a nearby chair as the music crescendos and the curtain falls.

END OF ACT I

ACT II

At the end of Music Song #14, a tremolo is held while CLARENCE and JOSEPH enter and speak over the tremolo. Clarence, ever the eager one, immediately quizzes Joseph.

CLARENCE: Well Joseph, did Mary get Uncle Billy on the phone? Did she find George? Is he okay?

JOSEPH: Patience, Clarence, patience. You'll find out in due time.

CLARENCE: So, where did George run off to?

Tremolo ends.

JOSEPH: He went straight to Old Man Potter's office.

CLARENCE: Old Man Potter? Why would he go to him?

JOSEPH: You'll see, Clarence. Just watch and you'll see. George was clearly desperate.

SCENE 1

POTTER'S OFFICE

Lights fade up on Potter's Office. POTTER is seated at his desk, his GOON is beside him. GEORGE is seated in a chair across the desk from him, without a hat or coat.

GEORGE: I'm in trouble, Mr. Potter. I need help. Through some sort of an accident, my company's short in their accounts. The bank examiner's up there today. I've got to raise eight thousand dollars immediately.

POTTER *(casually)*: Oh, so that's what the reporters wanted to talk to you about?

GEORGE *(incredulous)*: The reporters?

POTTER: Yes. They called me up from your Building and Loan. Oh, there's a man over there from the D.A.'s office, too. He's looking for you.

GEORGE *(desperate)*: Please help me, Mr. Potter. Help me, won't you, please? Can't you see what it means to my family? I'll pay you any sort of a bonus on the loan... any interest. If you still want the Building and Loan, why I...

POTTER *(interrupting)*: George, could it possibly be there's a slight discrepancy in the books?

GEORGE: No, sir. There's nothing wrong with the books. I've just misplaced eight thousand dollars. I can't find it anywhere.

POTTER: You misplaced eight thousand dollars?

GEORGE: Yes, sir.

POTTER: Have you notified the police?

GEORGE: No, sir. I didn't want the publicity. Harry's homecoming is tomorrow.

POTTER: What've you been doing, George? Playing the market with the company's money?

GEORGE: No, sir. No, sir. I haven't.

POTTER: What is it— a woman then? You know, it's all over town that you've been giving money to Violet Bick.

GEORGE *(incredulous)*: What?

POTTER: Not that it makes any difference to me, but why did you come to me? Why don't you go to the riff-raff you love so well? Or what about your good friend, Sam Wainwright?

GEORGE: I can't get a hold of him. He's in Europe.

POTTER: Well, what about all your other friends?

GEORGE: They don't have that kind of money, Mr. Potter. You know that. You're the only one in town that can help me.

POTTER: I see. I've suddenly become quite important. What kind of security would I have, George? Have you got any stocks?

GEORGE *(shaking his head)*: No, sir.

POTTER: Bonds? Real estate? Collateral of any kind?

GEORGE *(pulls out policy)*: I have some life insurance, a fifteen thousand dollar policy.

POTTER: Yes... how much is your equity in it?

GEORGE *(almost ashamed)*: Five hundred dollars.

POTTER *(snickers indignantly)*: And you want eight thousand? *(Sarcastically)* Look at you. You used to be so cocky! You were going out and conquer the world! You once called me a warped, frustrated old man. Well what are you but a warped, frustrated young man? A miserable little clerk crawling in here on your hands and knees and begging for help. No securities. No stocks. No bonds. Nothing but a miserable little five hundred dollar equity in a life insurance policy. *(Chuckling)* George Bailey, you're worth more dead than alive!

GEORGE: I'll do anything Mr. Potter. I'll do anything for my wife and children. Please help me.

POTTER: I'll tell you what I'll do to help. Since the state examiner is still in town, as a stockholder of the Building and Loan, I'm going to swear out a warrant for your arrest.

GEORGE stands, numb from the assault.

And then I'm calling the district attorney. *(Getting louder)* Misappropriation of funds... manipulation... malfeasance!

GEORGE exits.

All right, George, go ahead. You can't hide in a little town like this. *(To his Goon)* Wheel me over to the phone and that's all for tonight.

SONG #15: POTTERSVILLE

> *As the music begins, The GOON wheels POTTER downstage and is joined by three other GOONS to form a "Goon Quartet". They are clearly "yes men" and frighteningly attentive to Potter's every movement and utterance.*

I wonder what life in Bedford Falls is going to be like without George Bailey?

(Singing)
ALL THE PEOPLE IN BEDFORD FALLS
ARE GONNA GROVEL AND BEG AND CRAWL
I WANT THE TOWN IN MY GREEDY PALM
I EVEN THINK IT MIGHT JUST GIVE ME A THRILL
TO NAME IT POTTERSVILLE

GOONS:
GEORGE WAS CARELESS

POTTER: He's a brainless dope!

GOONS:
LONG ON HIS DREAMIN' NOW SHORT ON HOPE
NOW THERE'S A NOOSE AT THE END OF HIS ROPE

POTTER:
IT WON'T BE LONG 'TIL I AM KING OF THE HILL

POTTER & GOONS:
RIGHT HERE IN POTTERSVILLE!

POTTER (speaks over music): So George, I'm a warped, frustrated old man. And you're worth more dead than alive!

> He laughs maniacally.

> (To the Goons)

Well, Boys?

GOONS (ad lib): Yes, Mr. Potter! Oh, you're right, Mr. Potter! Malfeasance! Misappropriation! Yes, Mr. Pot...!

> POTTER, who is practically bored at this point by their predictable agreement, rolls his eyes and cuts them off in mid-sentence as an orchestra conductor would using both hands. They stop abruptly, snapping back to attention.

POTTER:
ALL THE PEOPLE WHO SAY I'M A CURSE
MISUNDERSTAND ME, 'CAUSE I'M MUCH WORSE

GOONS:
HE'LL HAVE THEIR LIVES IN HIS CINCHED UP PURSE
HE'LL BUILD HIS DREAM AND THEN HE'LL
SLIP 'EM THE BILL
THEY'LL PAY IN POTTERSVILLE

POTTER:
IT WON'T BE LONG 'TIL I AM KING OF THE HILL
RIGHT HERE... HERE... HERE

GOONS:
RIGHT HERE... RIGHT HERE...

POTTER & GOON QUARTET:
HERE IN POTTERSVILLE.

> BLACKOUT. Music 15a. begins. CLARENCE and JOSEPH enter and speak during the change of scene.

SONG #15A: CHANGE OF SCENE – GEORGE ON BRIDGE

JOSEPH: And all the time, Potter had that eight thousand dollars in his desk drawer. It's still there, Clarence.

CLARENCE: But what about George, sir? Where is he?

JOSEPH: He went over to Martini's Bar. He had a couple of drinks, Clarence. Mr. Welch sat next to him at the bar.

CLARENCE: Who's Mr. Welch?

JOSEPH: He's the husband of Zuzu's teacher that George yelled at on the phone. Mr. Welch had a few drinks, too, and ended up hitting George right in the mouth.

CLARENCE: Oh dear. Is George alright?

> *GEORGE enters and the lights reveal a bridge unit, which is placed Down Center. The bridge railing is waist high and three crates (of graduated heights) are on the bridge under the railing. They look worn and discarded and have various bits of writing stamped on them (i.e., "vegetables", "canned goods" etc.). The crates will be used as step units for George during Music Song #15 to heighten the drama of the moments as he contemplates suicide. George crosses to the edge of the bridge unit, while not yet stepping on it.*

SCENE 2
THE BRIDGE

JOSEPH: Well, George left Martini's Bar five minutes ago, his mouth still bleeding from the punch he received. He's at the river now. On the bridge, looking at the water. Are you ready, Clarence?

CLARENCE: All ready, sir.

JOSEPH: Very well. Save George Bailey's life and you'll get your wings. You're on your own now, Clarence. Good luck.

CLARENCE: Thank you, Joseph.

> *CLARENCE and JOSEPH exit as GEORGE steps onto the bridge.*

GEORGE: God... dear Father in Heaven, I'm not a praying man, but if you're up there and you can hear me, show me the way.

> *Music 15a. segues into the introduction of Music 16.*

SONG #16: EVERY DREAM I EVER DREAMED

> *(Almost delirious)*

Mary... Mary... I'm worth more dead than alive. I love you kids. I love you, Mary.

> *(Singing)*
YOU WERE THERE BESIDE ME, GOLDEN IN THE SUN
LONG AGO WHEN LOVE WAS NEW
CAPTURED IN MY MEMORY, BEAUTIFUL AND YOUNG
EVERY DREAM I EVER DREAMED WAS YOU

IF I HAD BUT ONE WISH UPON A SHOOTING STAR
BEFORE MY DAYS ON EARTH WERE THROUGH
I'D GIVE TEN THOUSAND LIFETIMES
FOR A MOMENT IN YOUR ARMS
EVERY DREAM I EVER DREAMED WAS YOU

AND EVEN IF I'M FAR, FAR AWAY
WHEN YOU FEEL THE WIND ON YOUR FACE
KNOW THAT I'M NEXT TO YOU

> *During the interlude, GEORGE hears his own voice in his head repeating the words he spoke earlier to UNCLE BILLY, haunting him as he becomes all the more focused on his suicide.*

GEORGE'S VOICE: Do you realize what this means? It means bankruptcy and scandal, and prison! That's what it means! That's what it means!

> *CLARENCE enters opposite GEORGE, unseen by George. Clarence is lit by a soft light, dressed in white, practically glowing with an angelic hue. His eyes are fixed on George as he crosses slowly toward the bridge. George steps onto the first crate, positioning himself to jump as the music crescendos. As George takes that first step, Clarence stops, as if paralyzed in disbelief that George is going to follow through with his suicide.*

GEORGE:

WHEN COLORS OF THE TWILIGHT FADE INTO THE DARK

THIS ONE THING I SWEAR IS TRUE

> *GEORGE steps higher onto the next crate.*

NO ONE EVER HELD YOU DEEPER IN HIS HEART

EVERY DREAM I EVER DREAMED WAS YOU

I WOULD WALK A THOUSAND MILES

> *GEORGE steps onto the highest crate positioned against the bridge railing. With outstretched arms, he sings the final, soaring lines:*

GIVE MY LIFE TO SEE YOU SMILE

EVERY DREAM I EVER DREAMED WAS YOU

> *BLACKOUT.*

> *Water splashing SFX is heard. GEORGE exits.*

SONG #16A: UNDERSCORE – AFTER EVERY DREAM

> *Near the end of Music 16a., CLARENCE and JOSEPH's voices are heard over the music, offstage.*

JOSEPH'S VOICE: That was pretty fast thinking, Clarence... jumping in the water so that George would save you.

CLARENCE'S VOICE *(breathless)*: That's George Bailey, sir. Always thinking about others. Even when he's at the darkest time of his life.

JOSEPH'S VOICE: Good job. You may get those wings yet.

CLARENCE'S VOICE *(still breathless)*: I hope so, sir.

JOSEPH'S VOICE: Now pull George up to dry land beside the bridge and get to work.

> *The lights fade up revealing GEORGE and CLARENCE standing next to the bridge. There is blood on George's mouth.*

GEORGE: You almost drowned there, old fellow. How did you fall in?

CLARENCE: I didn't fall in. I jumped in to save you, George.

GEORGE looks up, surprised.

GEORGE: You what? To save me?

CLARENCE: Well, I did, didn't I? You didn't go through with it, did you?

GEORGE: Go through with what?

CLARENCE: Suicide.

GEORGE: Where do you come from?

CLARENCE: Heaven. I had to act quickly, that's why I jumped in. I knew if you thought I was drowning you'd try to save me. And you did. And that's how I saved you.

GEORGE *(offhand)*: Very funny.

CLARENCE: Your lip's bleeding, George.

GEORGE's hand goes to his mouth.

GEORGE: Yeah, well, I was over at the bar before you decided to take a swim and I got busted in the jaw by an irate teacher's husband.

CLARENCE: Oh really?

GEORGE *(casually interested)*: How do you know my name?

CLARENCE: Oh, I know all about you. I've watched you grow up from a little boy.

GEORGE: Well, who are you then?

CLARENCE: Clarence Oddbody, A— S— 2.

GEORGE: Clarence Oddbody, A— S— 2? What's the A— S— 2?

CLARENCE: Angel, Second Class.

GEORGE: Hey, what's with you? Wonder what Martini put in those drinks. Now look here. Why did you want to save me?

CLARENCE: Because I'm your guardian angel, George.

GEORGE *(humoring him)*: Oh, I see. Well, you look like about the kind of angel I'd get. *(Sarcastically)* What happened to your wings?

CLARENCE: I haven't won my wings yet. That's why I'm an angel Second Class. But you can help me earn them, George, by letting me help you.

GEORGE: Oh. Well, you don't happen to have eight thousand bucks on you?

CLARENCE: Oh no, no. We don't use money in Heaven.

GEORGE: Oh, that's right, I keep forgetting. Comes in pretty handy down here, bub. I found it out a little late. I'm worth more dead than alive.

CLARENCE: Now look, you mustn't talk like that. I won't get my wings with that attitude. You just don't know all you've done. If it hadn't been for you...

GEORGE *(interrupting)*: Yeah, if it hadn't been for me, everybody'd be a lot better off. My wife, my kids, my friends.

CLARENCE *(looking up toward Heaven)*: Oh, this isn't going to be easy.

GEORGE: They'd all be better off if I hadn't been born.

CLARENCE: What did you say?

GEORGE: I said I wish I'd never been born!

> *GEORGE rises angrily and turns his back to the audience. As CLARENCE steps in front of him, George pulls his coat up on his shoulders up a bit, while he simultaneously and casually wipes the blood from his lip. This motion should be hidden from the audience.*

CLARENCE: You mustn't say things like that. You... *(Getting an idea)* Hey, wait a minute. George, that's wonderful.

GEORGE *(turning around)*: Wonderful? What's wonderful?

CLARENCE: The idea you just gave me.

> *CLARENCE faces front and snaps his finger as Music Song #16b. underscores the finger snap. A lighting change indicates the world is different now.*

SONG #16B: PRESTO

Well, you've got your wish. You've never been born.

GEORGE: Never been born?

CLARENCE: Exactly. No worries. No eight thousand dollars to get... nothing. You simply don't exist.

GEORGE *(humoring him again)*: Okay, alright. Whatever you say.

CLARENCE: George, I can do things. Strange things. I can show you the world the way it would be if you hadn't been born.

GEORGE *(jiggling a finger in his bad ear)*: Hey, wait a minute. This ear of mine. Say something else in that bad ear.

CLARENCE: You don't have a bad ear anymore. I don't think you're concentrating. Don't you see? You're not the George Bailey you think you are. You're... well, you're nobody.

GEORGE *(still amazed with his ear)*: Well that's the doggonedest thing... I haven't heard anything out of that ear since I was a kid.

CLARENCE: Your lip's stopped bleeding, too.

> *GEORGE licks his lip, then feels it.*

GEORGE *(puzzled)*: Yeah. Say, what's happening here? What is this anyway? *(Changing his thinking)* I need a drink, that's what I need. What about you, angel? You want a drink?

CLARENCE: I don't think angels are supposed to drink.

GEORGE: C'mon, we'll go as soon as our clothes are dry.

CLARENCE: Our clothes are dry, George.

GEORGE *(feeling the clothing)*: Hey, so they are. That's funny. Look, let's put these on and then we'll stroll over to Martini's and then... oh, excuse me, I'll stroll and you'll fly.

CLARENCE: I don't have my wings yet.

GEORGE *(humoring him still)*: Oh, that's right. I forgot. Well, a couple of drinks and we'll both fly.

SONG #16C: CHANGE OF SCENE – INTO POTTERSVILLE

> *The lights fade as GEORGE and CLARENCE exit. The scene change reveals Main Street. There is a statue (optional) of MR. POTTER placed center. Several citizens enter but pay no attention to George or Clarence. George stops one of the passersby and addresses him.*

SCENE 3

MAIN STREET

GEORGE: Say, where's Martini's bar?

PASSERBY: I beg your pardon?

GEORGE: There used to be a bar over there named Martini's and now it's gone.

PASSERBY: There's never been a bar named Martini's here in Pottersville.

GEORGE *(blankly)*: Pottersville? You mean Bedford Falls.

PASSERBY: I mean Pottersville. *(Sharply)* Don't you think I know where I live? What's the matter with you?

> *The introduction to Music Song #17 begins.*

GEORGE *(confused)*: Pottersville?

> *The PASSERBY turns sharply and joins the other shabbily-clad residents of Pottersville gathering to sing. POTTERSVILLIANS 1 & 2 are street vendors selling socks, Downstage Right.*
>
> *GEORGE and CLARENCE cross to Stage Left and sit to watch the presentation. As the POTTERSVILLIANS sing, they pay irreverent, mock tribute to the statue of Potter placed center.*

POTTERSVILLIAN 1: Look around you. All we're missin' is castle walls and parasols.

POTTERSVILLIAN 2: Yeah, and gondolas... it's Henry Potter's dream.

POTTERSVILLIAN 1: Uh huh. And one man's dream is another man's nightmare.

SONG #17: SWELL

POTTERSVILLIANS 1 & 2:
GEE, MR. POTTER, YOU'RE SWELL
WE BUBBLE IN YOUR CAULDRON
UNDERNEATH YOUR SPELL
YOU ARE JUST A CANNIBAL
DROOLIN' AT THE DINNERBELL
GEE, MR. POTTER, YOU'RE SWELL

POTTERSVILLIAN 1 *(sarcastically)*: Swell.

POTTERSVILLIAN 2 *(with mock sincerity)*: Yeah, swell, Mr. Potter.

POTTERSVILLIANS 1 & 2:
GEE, MR. POTTER, YOU'RE SWELL
THE AROMA OF YOUR SPIRIT
HAS A TRUE DISTINCTIVE SMELL

POTTERSVILLIAN 1:
KINDA LIKE AN OUTHOUSE WHEN
THE SUMMER'S HOT AS...

> *At that moment, several women cross the stage.*

POTTERSVILLIANS 1 & 2 *(speaking; emphasizing the syllable "Hell")*: HELL-o, ladies!

POTTERSVILLIAN 2:
GEE, MR. POTTER, YOU'RE SWELL

> *The women who crossed to the street vendors stop to join the revelry.*

POTTERSVILLIANS 1, 2 & WOMEN:
YOUR HEART TO GREED HAS SUCCUMBED
LIKE THE HAIR FROM YOUR HEAD FATE HAS PLUCKED IT.
THE DIFFERENCE BETWEEN YOU AND A BUCKET OF POND SCUM

POTTERSVILLIAN 1 *(disgusted)*: Is simply... the bucket.

ALL POTTERSVILLIANS *(dancing a simple soft shoe routine)*:
GEE, MR. POTTER, YOU'RE SWELL
YOU PUT US ALL IN SHACKS LIKE
RATS IN PRISON CELLS
THEN ACT AS THOUGH THE SHANTY
IS A HOLLYWOOD HOTEL

ALL POTTERSVILLIANS:
GEE, MR. POTTER, YOU'RE SWELL

POTTERSVILLIAN 3: He's built his dream here.

POTTERSVILLIAN 4: Yeah, and he's slipped us the bill.

ALL POTTERSVILLIANS:
GEE, MR. POTTER, YOU'RE SWELL!

POTTERSVILLIAN 1 *(sarcastically)*: Swell.

> *After the song, the crowd disperses and exits. A few remain to chat with each other. A lonely Salvation Army bell ringer stands next to a kettle and no one is giving nor paying attention to her.*

GEORGE: What's going on here? Everything has changed here.

CLARENCE: All of Bedford Falls has changed. You're having your wish, George. You've never been born. Oh, there will be lots of things you've never seen before.

> *CLARENCE suddenly notices the Salvation Army bell ringer.*

> *(To George)*

Oh, excuse me.

He crosses to the kettle and drops in a coin. The Salvation Army bell ringer rings the bell apathetically.

CLARENCE (CONT'D): Oh, good. Somebody just made it!

GEORGE: Made what?

CLARENCE: Every time a bell rings it means another angel just got his wings.

GEORGE: What? Are you crazy?

> *MR. GOWER enters staggering down the street toward GEORGE and CLARENCE. He is obviously a broken-down panhandler; his hat in his hand.*
>
> *GEORGE rushes up to him.*

Mr. Gower! Mr. Gower!

> *MR. GOWER stares blankly at GEORGE.*

Don't you know me? This is George Bailey!

MR. GOWER *(drunken):* Will you buy me a drink, mister? Just one drink?

PASSERBY: That rumhead spent twenty years in jail for poisoning a kid. If you know him, you must be a jailbird yourself. I'm calling a cop on you.

> *The PASSERBY exits. MR. GOWER staggers off stage.*

GEORGE *(calling after Mr. Gower):* Mr. Gower! Mr. Gower!

CLARENCE: He doesn't know you, George. You see, you weren't there to stop him from putting poison into that prescription.

GEORGE: What do you mean I wasn't there? Look... what are you? Are you a hypnotist?

CLARENCE: No, of course not.

GEORGE: Well then, why am I seeing all these strange things?

CLARENCE: Don't you understand? It's because you were never born.

GEORGE: Then if I wasn't born, who am I?

> *GEORGE reaches frantically for his wallet.*

CLARENCE: Your wallet isn't there, George. You're nobody. You have no identity. No papers, no cards, no driver's license, no insurance policy.

> *GEORGE frantically checks his pant pockets.*

They're not there, either.

GEORGE: What?

CLARENCE: Zuzu's petals. You've been given a great gift, George. A chance to see what the world would be like if you'd never been born.

GEORGE *(angrily):* You're crazy. You're crazy as a bed bug and you're driving me crazy, too. Now look, I'm going home to my wife and family. Do you understand that? And I'm going home alone!

SONG #17A: CHANGE OF SCENE – INTO GRANVILLE HOUSE

> *GEORGE exits. CLARENCE crosses Downstage as JOSEPH speaks, voice over Music 17a.*

JOSEPH'S VOICE: Better not leave him alone, Clarence. Keep following him.

CLARENCE: Yes, Joseph... I'll stay near him, sir.

JOSEPH'S VOICE: What do you see, Clarence?

CLARENCE *(looking over the audience's heads, as if seeing the action)*: Poor George. He's seeing more of Main Street now, the way it is without his life. The thing that's really shocked him is the old Building and Loan office. It's a pawn shop now.

JOSEPH'S VOICE: What's he doing now, Clarence? Can you see?

CLARENCE: The taxi driver, Ernie Bishop, is taking him home. Yes... he's getting out now and going up to the old Granville House where he lived there all those years.

JOSEPH'S VOICE: You'd better tag along, Clarence.

CLARENCE: Oh, I will, sir. I will!

> *CLARENCE crosses to the Granville house.*

SCENE 4

THE GRANVILLE HOUSE

Music Song #17a. ends as the lights fade up on the Granville House. GEORGE stands inside, looking around frantically. It is deserted and desolate. ERNIE stands nearby. George turns to Ernie.

GEORGE: Look here, Ernie, straighten me out here. I've got some bad liquor or something. Listen to me now. Now, you are Ernie Bishop, and you live in Bailey Park with your wife and kid. That's right isn't it?

ERNIE *(suspiciously)*: You seen my wife?

GEORGE *(exasperated)*: Seen your wife?! I've been to your house a hundred times!

ERNIE: Look bud, what's the idea? I live in a shack in Potter's Field and my wife ran away three years ago and took the kid... and I ain't never seen you before in my life. Now pay me my cab fare and I'm gettin' outta here.

GEORGE ignores him and walks around the house frantically.

GEORGE: Mary! Mary! Tommy! Pete! Janie! Zuzu! Where are you?

CLARENCE crosses to GEORGE.

CLARENCE: They're not here, George. It's just an old, abandoned house. You have no wife or children.

GEORGE turns sharply now seeing CLARENCE.

GEORGE: What have you done to them?

BERT enters and crosses quickly to GEORGE with his gun drawn.

BERT: All right, put up your hands. No fast moves... both of you.

GEORGE: Bert! Thank heaven you're here!

He rushes toward BERT.

BERT: Stand back!

GEORGE: Bert, what's happened to this house? Where's Mary? Where's my kids?

BERT: Look, now why don't you be a good guy and I'll take you in to a doctor. Everything's going to be all right.

GEORGE: Bert... now listen to me. Ernie, will you take me over to my mother's house? Bert, listen! It's this fellow here... he says he's an angel... he's tried to hypnotize me.

BERT: I hate to do this fellow...

BERT raises his gun to strike GEORGE on the head. CLARENCE darts in and fixes his teeth in Bert's wrist.

Ow! Ouch!

> *ERNIE grabs CLARENCE by the shoulders and shakes him.*

ERNIE: Let go of him!

CLARENCE: Run, George, Run, George!

> *As GEORGE runs away, CLARENCE finally lets go of BERT's wrist.*

BERT: Come back here!

> *ERNIE and BERT run a few steps after GEORGE but it's too late; George has escaped. As Bert and Ernie turn back towards CLARENCE, he snaps his fingers (the finger snap is underscored by Music Song #17b). As he snaps his fingers, he moves quickly Upstage of them.*

SONG #17B: PRESTO (REPRISE)

> *Suddenly, ERNIE and BERT can't see CLARENCE anymore.*

Where'd he go? He was right over there.

ERNIE *(stammering)*: I... I need a drink.

> *BLACKOUT*

SONG #18: CHANGE OF SCENE – INTO MAIN STREET

> *CLARENCE crosses to Downstage Center as the scene changes and is lit in a single spotlight as he speaks to JOSEPH. Joseph's voice is heard over Music Song #18.*

JOSEPH'S VOICE: Clarence! You're by yourself again. Where's George?

CLARENCE: He's at his mother's house, sir.

JOSEPH'S VOICE: Well, if George hasn't been born, he has no mother.

CLARENCE: Oh, he's being very stubborn, sir. He'll just have to find these things out for himself.

JOSEPH'S VOICE: But his mother! That's a terribly bitter blow to a man... his own mother not knowing him.

CLARENCE: You mean I shouldn't have let him...

JOSEPH'S VOICE: I mean you'd better find him right away. Oh, and stop biting policemen, Clarence.

CLARENCE: It almost didn't work, sir. My teeth aren't quite what they used to be! *(To himself)* There must be some easier way for me to get my wings.

> *CLARENCE turns around and the lights fade up to reveal GEORGE standing on Main Street, looking lost and disoriented. There is a simple park bench placed Left Center.*

SCENE 5

MAIN STREET

CLARENCE: I'm here again, George.

GEORGE *(still shocked)*: My mother. My own mother didn't know me. If only Harry were here. If only he was back from Washington.

CLARENCE: Your brother fell through the ice and was drowned at the age of nine.

GEORGE: That's a lie! He went to war! He got the Congressional Medal of Honor! He saved the life of every man on that transport.

CLARENCE: Every man on that transport died. Harry wasn't there to save them because you weren't there to save Harry. Strange, isn't it? Each man's life touches so many other lives. You see, George, you really had a wonderful life. Don't you see what a mistake it would be to throw it away?

GEORGE: Clarence...

CLARENCE: Yes, George?

GEORGE: Where's Mary? Please, where's my wife?

CLARENCE: I'm... not supposed to tell. You're not going to like it.

GEORGE *(desperately, grabbing Clarence by his lapels)*: Where's Mary? Where is she?

CLARENCE: She's an old maid. She never married.

GEORGE: Where is she?

CLARENCE: She's just about to close up the library!

> *GEORGE lets go and rushes out. Music Song #19 begins.*

> *(Collecting himself)*

Oh, Joseph. This is awfully hard on poor George. But I know it's best for him. You know, he did have a wonderful life. If he and all these humans down here would just realize what a gift life really is.

> *CLARENCE crosses to sit on the park bench.*

SONG #19: THOSE MOMENTS

> *(Singing)*
> EVERY DAY SLIPS AWAY
> AND DISAPPEARS ONCE AGAIN
> LIKE THE SAND THROUGH OUR HANDS
> SWEPT AWAY ON THE WIND
> CLARENCE

CLARENCE (CONT'D):
HOLD ON TO THOSE MOMENTS WHEN BELLS FROM CATHEDRALS
RING CROSS AN AUTUMN DAY
HOLD ON TO THOSE MOMENTS WHEN GREEN FIELDS OF CLOVER
GROW WHERE THE CHILDREN PLAY
HOLD ON TO THOSE NIGHTS WHEN STARS BLAZE ABOVE
CLING TO THE FEELING OF FEELING IN LOVE
SEIZE EVERY MOMENT ALL YOUR LIFE LONG
BEFORE THOSE MOMENTS ARE GONE

WE ARE YOUNG THEN WE'RE OLD
AND ALL BETWEEN SEEMS TO FLY
SUMMERS COME AND WINTERS GO
HOW THE SEASONS RACE BY

HOLD ON TO THOSE MOMENTS WHEN BELLS FROM CATHEDRALS
RING CROSS AN AUTUMN DAY
HOLD ON TO THOSE MOMENTS WHEN GREEN FIELDS OF CLOVER
GROW WHERE THE CHILDREN PLAY
HOLD ON TO THOSE NIGHTS WHEN STARS BLAZE ABOVE
CLING TO THE FEELING OF FEELING IN LOVE
SEIZE EVERY MOMENT ALL YOUR LIFE LONG
BEFORE THOSE MOMENTS ARE GONE

SEIZE EVERY MOMENT ALL YOUR LIFE LONG
BEFORE THOSE MOMENTS ARE GONE

> *After the song, JOSEPH speaks to interrupt CLARENCE's*
> *frame of mind.*

JOSEPH'S VOICE: Well, Clarence, where's George now? You let him get away again.

CLARENCE *(collecting himself)*: Oh, I'm sorry sir! Well, I'll try to see him.

> *The lights on stage fade up, again revealing Main Street.*
> *CLARENCE remains Downstage Center, straining his eyes,*
> *looking over the audience's heads as if to see GEORGE and*
> *the current action.*

He's starting to come in, sir. Yes, there he is. Oh, dear. He did find Mary at the library. And he's following her home. She's continuing to walk, pretending he's not there.

> *MARY enters Stage Left, crossing the stage. GEORGE is*
> *following closely behind. She is very different... no buoyancy*
> *in her walk, none of her abandon and love of life.*

> *She is wearing glasses and a hat. CLARENCE crosses to Stage Right to watch the action. Introduction to Music Song #20 begins.*

GEORGE: Mary! It's George! Don't you know me? What's happened to us?

MARY *(stopping, turning to him)*: I don't know you, sir.

GEORGE *(desperately)*: Please, Mary. Please listen to me!

> *GEORGE begins to sing. During the song, a small crowd gathers around, noticing the commotion.*

SONG #20: DON'T YOU RECOGNIZE ME?

(Singing)
DON'T YOU RECOGNIZE ME, MARY?
DON'T YOU KNOW ME ANYMORE?
DON'T YOU UNDERSTAND THAT
I AM YOUR SHELTER, I AM YOUR HOME
FROM THE RAFTERS TO THE FLOOR
DON'T YOU RECOGNIZE ME, MARY?
LOOK INTO MY EYES AND SEE
THAT I TRULY LOVE YOU, MARY
COME HOME TO ME!
DON'T YOU RECOGNIZE ME, MARY?

MAN: Leave that woman alone, mister!

GEORGE:
DON'T YOU KNOW ME ANYMORE?

WOMAN *(echoing the urgency)*: He needs a strait jacket!

> *BERT enters.*

GEORGE:
DON'T YOU UNDERSTAND THAT
I AM YOUR SHELTER, I AM YOUR HOME
FROM THE RAFTERS TO THE FLOOR
DON'T YOU RECOGNIZE ME, MARY?

MAN *(angrily)*: Somebody call the police!

GEORGE:
LOOK INTO MY EYES AND SEE

MARY *(desperately)*: I said I don't know you!

GEORGE *(not giving up)*:
THAT I TRULY LOVE YOU, MARY
COME HOME TO ME!

> *GEORGE grabs MARY by her shoulders.*

GEORGE (CONT'D):
DON'T YOU RECOGNIZE ME, MARY?
LOOK INTO MY EYES AND SEE
THAT I TRULY LOVE YOU, MARY
COME HOME TO ME!

> *MARY screams, breaks away from GEORGE and runs to the side of one of the crowd members whom she knows and comforts her. A man from the crowd restrains George.*

SONG #20A: UNDERSCORE (AFTER DON'T YOU RECOGNIZE ME?)

> *(Wildly, speaking)*

Mary! Don't run away!

MARY *(to Bert)*: That man... stop him! He's a lunatic!

GEORGE: Tom! Ed! Charlie! That's my wife!

> *MARY screams again, then faints into the arms of the person comforting her.*

Clarence! Clarence! Where are you!

BERT: Oh, it's you!

> *BERT grabs for GEORGE, who punches Bert right in the mouth, knocking him down. George runs off stage yelling for CLARENCE.*

GEORGE: Clarence! Clarence! I need you!

BERT *(collecting himself and standing up)*: After him!

SONG #20B: SCENE CHANGE – INTO BRIDGE

> *Lights fade as BERT leads the throng with his gun drawn following GEORGE. CLARENCE again steps to Downstage Center and speaks during the change of scene.*

JOSEPH'S VOICE: Clarence!

CLARENCE: Oh, where is George now, Joseph? I'm afraid I've lost him, sir.

JOSEPH'S VOICE: The mob is after him, Clarence. They think he was trying to hurt Mary.

CLARENCE: Joseph, I won't even get one wing out of this, will I? Let alone the deluxe halo.

JOSEPH'S VOICE: You have one more chance, Clarence. Look hard... look with your heart. Where do you see him?

> *CLARENCE begins to strain again, looking over the audience's heads. The lights fade up on the bridge as GEORGE enters, weary and disheveled, still half running from the chase he's just endured.*

SCENE 6

THE BRIDGE

CLARENCE: He's coming in, sir! And it looks as if the mob has lost him. I'm going to the bridge now.

JOSEPH'S VOICE: Hurry, Clarence! Hurry!

CLARENCE: I will, Joseph!

> *CLARENCE exits. GEORGE steps onto the bridge. Music Song #20a. segues into Music Song #21.*

GEORGE: Clarence! Clarence! Where are you? Help me, Clarence. Get me back. I don't care what happens to me. Only get me back to my wife and kids. Clarence, please. Please! I want to live again!

> *GEORGE bows his head and clasps his hands. Lights reveal MARY (preferably behind a scrim, elevated and unseen to George). She is holding the phone (after having hung it up from UNCLE BILLY).*

SONG #21: EVERY DREAM I EVER DREAMED (REPRISE)

MARY:
IF I HAD BUT ONE WISH
UPON A SHOOTING STAR
BEFORE MY DAYS ON EARTH WERE THROUGH
I'D GIVE TEN THOUSAND LIFETIMES
FOR A MOMENT IN YOUR ARMS
> *(Speaking)*

Every dream I've ever dreamed was you.
> *(Singing)*

AND EVEN IF I'M FAR, FAR AWAY
WHEN YOU FEEL THE WIND ON YOUR FACE
KNOW THAT I'M NEXT TO YOU

GEORGE: I want to live again. I want to live again. Please, God, let me live again.

MARY:
EVERY DREAM I EVER DREAMED WAS YOU.
> *The light on MARY fades.*

GEORGE *(almost whispered)*: Please, God, let me live again.

> *BERT enters and runs onto the bridge.*

BERT: Hey, George! You all right?

GEORGE *(warningly)*: Now get out of here, Bert, or I'll hit you again! Get out!

BERT: What the Sam Hill you yelling for, George?

GEORGE: Don't... George?

> *GEORGE touches BERT unbelievingly.*

Bert, do you know me?

BERT: Know you? Are you kiddin'? I've been looking all over town trying to find you. Where you been? Hey, your mouth's bleeding, are you sure you're all right?

> *GEORGE touches his lips with his tongue, wipes the upstage side of his mouth with his hand and laughs happily. His rapture knows no bounds.*

GEORGE *(joyously)*: My mouth's bleeding! Bert, my mouth's bleed... *(Feeling in his pocket)* Zuzu's petals! Zuzu's... they're here Bert! What do you know about that! Merry Christmas!

> *He gives a bear hug to an astonished BERT. Music Song #22 begins. The scene change reveals Main Street in Bedford Falls where many townspeople are gathered.*

SCENE 7

MAIN STREET

GEORGE *(looking around frantically):* Mary! Mary! *(Yelling joyously as he darts back and forth, up and down the stage)* Yeah! Hello, Bedford Falls! Merry Christmas movie house! Merry Christmas you wonderful old Building and Loan!

SONG #22: I AM HOME (REPRISE II)

> *(Singing)*
> THIS QUIET TOWN IS QUAINT AND FAIR
> SNOW COVERED ROOF TOPS AND CHARMING FLARE
> THE MAIN STREET SOUNDS DRIFT ON THE AIR
> AS LONG AS I AM THERE I AM HOME

ALL:
> IT IS THE SHELTER THAT COVERS ME
> IT IS THE WINDOW THAT OPENS TO THE WORLD I SEE
> AND I THANK THE STARS ABOVE, FOR THE PEOPLE THAT I LOVE
> WHEN I'M IN THIS TOWN, IN MY HEART I'VE FOUND
> I AM HOME!

> *GEORGE has created quite a commotion and more TOWNSPEOPLE are starting to enter from various parts of the house and sing, including MR. GOWER and BERT.*

GEORGE: Merry Christmas!

TOWNSPEOPLE *(ad lib):* Merry Christmas, George! Good to see you!

MR. GOWER:
> IN BEDFORD FALLS THE SHADOWS RUN
> ACROSS FRONT PORCHES WHEN TWILIGHT COMES

BERT:
> THE SKY IS DEEP AND WIDE AND CLEAR
> AS LONG AS I AM HERE I AM HOME.

ALL:
> IT IS THE SHELTER THAT COVERS ME
> IT IS THE WINDOW THAT OPENS TO THE WORLD I SEE
> AND I THANK THE STARS ABOVE, FOR THE PEOPLE WHOM I LOVE
> LIVE HERE ALL AROUND, WHEN I'M IN THIS TOWN
> I AM HOME!

GEORGE:
> THE BANDSTAND ON THE COURTHOUSE SQUARE
> GAZEBOS PEPPERED EVERYWHERE
> THE LILIES IN THE PARK IN SUMMERTIME

GEORGE (CONT'D):
   THE CHIMNEY SMOKE WHEN WINTER WAKES
   THE WAY THE GEESE FLY O'ER THE LAKES
   I KNOW WITHOUT A DOUBT IT'S PARADISE
ALL:
   IT IS THE SHELTER THAT COVERS ME
   IT IS THE WINDOW THAT OPENS TO THE WORLD I SEE
   AND I THANK THE STARS ABOVE, FOR THE PEOPLE WHOM I LOVE
   LIVE HERE ALL AROUND, WHEN I'M IN THIS TOWN
   I AM HOME!

> *At the end of the song, MARY enters and runs up to GEORGE, covering him with hugs and kisses. The children cling to George.*

GEORGE: Merry Christmas, Bedford Falls!

ALL: Merry Christmas, George!

MARY: Where've you been? We looked all over town for you, darling.

GEORGE *(continuing to hug her)*: Let me touch you! Oh, you're real!

BANK EXAMINER: Uh, Mr. Bailey, I hate to interrupt but I'm afraid we have some business to discuss.

GEORGE: Well, hello, Mr. Bank Examiner!

> *He grabs his hand and shakes it.*

BANK EXAMINER *(solemnly)*: Mr. Bailey, I'm afraid there's a deficit.

GEORGE: I know. Eight thousand dollars.

BANK EXAMINER *(reaching in his coat)*: I've got a paper for you from the sheriff.

GEORGE *(happily)*: I'll bet it's a warrant for my arrest. Isn't it wonderful? Merry Christmas!

MARY: You have no idea what's happened, George! It's a miracle... it's a miracle!

> *MARY turns to the crowd and summons UNCLE BILLY.*

Uncle Billy! Bring it out!

> *UNCLE BILLY, who has been hidden by the crowd, steps forward carrying a laundry basket overflowing with money. The crowd applauds.*

UNCLE BILLY: Isn't it wonderful!

> *He places the basket Downstage Center.*

Mary did it, George! She told a few people you were in trouble and they scattered all over town collecting money.

UNCLE BILLY (CONT'D): They didn't ask any questions... just said: "If George is in trouble count on me." You've never seen anything like it!

> *The crowd heartily ad libs agreement.*

MARY: And that's not all, George.

> *She holds up a slip of paper.*

This is a telegram from London. *(Reading)* "Mr. Gower cables you need cash. Stop. My office instructed to advance you up to twenty-five thousand dollars. Stop. Hee-haw and Merry Christmas. Sam Wainwright."

> *The crowd cheers and MARY drops the telegram on the pile of money. HARRY, in Naval uniform, enters.*

HARRY: Hello, George!

GEORGE: Harry... Harry!

> *They embrace.*

But what about your awards banquet in New York?

HARRY: Oh, I left in right in the middle of it as soon as I got Mary's telegram. I wanted to be here with you, George... *(Looking at the money basket, then indicating the crowd)* the richest man in town!

> *The crowd cheers. GEORGE picks up ZUZU. He puts his arm around MARY and their other children gather around them as everyone joyously sings (a cappella).*

SONG #22A: AULD LANG SYNE

ALL *(a cappella)*:
SHOULD OLD ACQUAINTANCE BE FORGOT
AND NEVER BROUGHT TO MIND,
SHOULD OLD ACQUAINTANCE BE FORGOT
AND DAYS OF AULD LANG SYNE.
FOR AULD LANG SYNE, MY DEAR.
FOR AULD LANG SYNE.
WE'LL TAKE A CUP OF KINDNESS, YET.
FOR AULD LANG SYNE.

MARY *(picking up a book in the money basket)*: Look, darling. Someone put a book in here. How sweet! *(Looking at the cover and reading the title)* "The Adventures of Tom Sawyer". *(Opening the book)* And something's written in it.

> *She gives the book to GEORGE. As George reads, CLARENCE enters upstage, looking proudly over the proceedings. The others on stage cannot see him. He now has small "baby wings" but they are unseen by the audience until he reveals them shortly.*

GEORGE *(reading the inscription)*: "Dear George, remember no man is a failure who has friends. Thanks for the wings. Love, Clarence."

MARY: Clarence? Who's that?

GEORGE: That's a Christmas present from a very dear friend of mine.

At that moment, we hear church bells chime.

MARY: Oh George... the cathedral bells... it's time for the Christmas Eve service.

ZUZU: Daddy, teacher says every time a bell rings, an angel gets his wings.

GEORGE *(smiling)*: That's right. That's right.

He looks up to the sky and winks.

Attaboy, Clarence. Attaboy!

CLARENCE happily salutes GEORGE, then whirls around, proudly revealing to the audience his new "baby" wings.

SONG #23: FINALE ULTIMO

ALL:
IT'S A WONDERFUL LIFE
IT'S REMARKABLY ASTOUNDING EVERY MINUTE
IT'S A WONDERFUL LIFE
IT'S A TREASURE AND A PLEASURE TO BE IN IT
FULL OF JOY AND REVELATION,
IT'S BEYOND IMAGINATION
AN INTOXICATING GIFT, EMPHATICALLY SUBLIME
IT'S A WONDERFUL, WONDERFUL LIFE
IT'S A WONDERFUL LIFE
IT'S A BEAUTIFUL AND BRILLIANT FLIGHT OF FANCY
IT'S A WONDERFUL LIFE
FULL OF FANTASY AND REVERIE AND DANCING
IT'S ENCHANTING AND DISARMING,
IT'S MYSTERIOUS AND CHARMING
IT'S A MESMERIZING WORLD, A DAZZ-E-LING SURPRISE
IT'S A WONDERFUL, WONDERFUL LIFE

AND WHEN THE SUN COMES UP
EACH DAY IS WORTH EXPLORING
LIKE ANGELS WITH NEW WINGS
I FEEL AS IF I'M SOARING

Waltz dance break.

ALL (CONT'D):
IT'S A WONDERFUL LIFE
FULL OF SHIMMERING UNENDING FASCINATION
IT'S A WONDERFUL LIFE
A MAGNIFICENT AND THRILLING CELEBRATION
IT'S THE DREAM THE HEART IS AFTER
OVERFLOWING WITH SWEET LAUGHTER
IT'S A RARE AND SPLENDID SONG
A MAGICAL DELIGHT
IT'S A WONDERFUL, WONDERFUL LIFE!

Blackout.

Lights up.

SONG #24: MUSIC FOR CURTAIN CALLS

HOLD ON TO THOSE MOMENTS WHEN BELLS FROM CATHEDRALS
RING CROSS AN AUTUMN DAY
HOLD ON TO THOSE MOMENTS WHEN GREEN FIELDS OF CLOVER
GROW WHERE THE CHILDREN PLAY
HOLD ON TO THOSE NIGHTS WHEN STARS BLAZE ABOVE
CLING TO THE FEELING OF FEELING IN LOVE
SEIZE EVERY MOMENT ALL YOUR LIFE LONG
BEFORE THOSE MOMENTS ARE GONE!

SONG #25: EXIT MUSIC

THE ENDSONG #1: OVERTURE

ABOUT STAGE RIGHTS

Based in Los Angeles and founded in 2000, Stage Rights is one of the foremost independent theatrical publishers in the United States, providing stage performance rights for a wide range of plays and musicals to theater companies, schools, and other producing organizations across the country and internationally. As a licensing agent, Stage Rights is committed to providing each producer the tools they need for financial and artistic success. Stage Rights is dedicated to the future of live theatre, offering special programs that champion new theatrical works.

To view all of our current plays and musicals, visit:
www.stagerights.com

Made in the USA
Coppell, TX
10 October 2021

63825786R00046